COOK IT. EAT IT. *Live it.*

The Everyday Joy of Food

by Jo Kenny

First published in South Africa by Kingsley Publishers, 2022
Copyright © Jo Kenny, 2022

The right of Jo Kenny to be identified as author of
this work has been asserted.

Kingsley Publishers
Pretoria, South Africa
www.kingsleypublishers.com

A catalogue copy of this book will be available from the National Library of South Africa
Hardcover ISBN: 978-0-620-95527-0
Paperback ISBN: 978-0-620-95526-3
eBook ISBN: 978-0-620-95528-7

To Alex, my husband and 'partner in food',
thank you for being the best damn
soulmate a food lover could ask for.
Life with you is forever sunny and delicious.

Introduction

I was just eight years old when my mum stood in front of the television one Sunday evening and announced, "Come on! It's time you learned how to cook."

I reluctantly followed her into the kitchen, where she proceeded to teach me how to make a simple chicken and rice dish. My mum showed me how much water and rice I would need to serve each person a portion. She taught me how to chop an onion and how long I had to fry it. I remember how much I enjoyed watching the little flecks of white flesh turn clear, and then golden in the pan. I knelt on a chair to reach the counter top and cut chicken into bite size pieces with scissors, and then I fried it with garlic and tarragon. Those weird pink cubes that I didn't recognise as food at first suddenly smelled like so many delicious meals I had enjoyed.

Never before then had I contemplated what on earth happened to create the food that appeared on my plate. I remember how incredibly proud I felt sitting down with my mum and dad to enjoy the dish that I helped to make. My reluctance to cook transformed into fascination.

After that day, 'the chicken and rice day', I began helping with more meals. As I entered secondary school it became common for me to cook for the family all by myself. In the beginning, what I served were horrific recreations of something I cobbled together for food technology class. At eleven years old my 'signature' dish (we'll use that term loosely), was a Fisherman's pie. It was awful - as bland and basic as you can imagine a child's first recipe to be. I made it with salty tinned tuna that hadn't been drained, soggy instant mash (yikes), and absolutely, categorically, not enough seasoning. My parents deserve a medal for choking it down.

That's how my journey into cooking began, but my entire life has been one big love affair revolving around food. I guess it's in my blood! As a small child I didn't exactly fit the stereotype of the fussy eater, I never needed cheering on to clear my plate or to try something new. Mealtimes were never a negotiation of how many bites were left before I could stop eating.

I was an unorthodox kid in restaurants too. I wasn't interested in chicken nuggets and chips, from the children's menu. I politely declined it in favour of 'proper' food. Even at the age of eight I would relish the very grown up feeling of ordering a fillet steak and seeing the waiter's eyebrows raise a little.

"Rare?" the waiter would politely repeat, looking to my parents for confirmation.

"Yes please!" I would confirm with a hungry grin and a nod.

Yep, I was definitely the kid who got remarks from her grandparents, saying things like, "Where do you put it?!"

In 2005 I met my now husband, Alex, or as I like to call him: my partner in food. Sharing my life with someone who loves to eat and cook was a must. We are true kindred spirits, both with an unwavering, unapologetic love of food, and all the delicious experiences that this world has to offer. The mixture of my hearty British cooking that I learned in childhood, and Alex's Guyanese family heritage, marries the external influences of our lives. We've managed to create our own world of delicious, vibrant food experiences that is unique to our home.

In 2012 I founded 'Girl Eats World', and for the best part of a decade my blog recorded my recipes and culinary stories. It began solely as a personal venture. I was encouraged by friends and family who grew tired of me documenting the meals I was eating, and posting it to Facebook. I needed a creative outlet. As the years passed, more people joined my corner of the internet, and now nothing makes me happier than seeing people from all over the country try my recipes. Alex can vouch for the squeals of excitement that happen whenever I see that a recipe of mine was tried, or a photo was shared.

I adore the online community that formed around my blog, but for me and many others there is no substitute for a physical recipe book. Practically speaking, electronic devices are asking for trouble when you bring them close to the cooking action, but it's not just that, there's an emotional aspect to it too. I still find something magical about a well-loved recipe book, one that over time gains the marks of the meals that it helped to make. Putting my recipes down on paper feels like the next natural step for me.

So there you go - a little snapshot of yours truly!

This book has been a dream of mine for years; a dream that I openly shared on my social media, and I am thrilled to finally offer the finished product. Those who know me already will be well acquainted with my quirks and general obsession with meal times. Thank you so much for following my journey into this new and exciting world of books. To those who are just getting acquainted with me, hello and welcome. It is always so very nice to meet a fellow food lover.

I dearly hope that this book will be the first of many. It is about sharing the absolute joy that food can bring to everyday life. My experiences and surroundings are shaped by vibrant, staple recipes and a happy food philosophy. I do hope that you enjoy this hearty collection of my favourite recipes, from my home to yours.

Contents

MEAT

BAKES AND DESSERTS

CUPBOARD STAPLES

If you rummage through my cupboards this is what you will always find. I love to use a wide variety of ingredients in my cooking, but for me these are the foundations. These are the basics that I feel naked without! Stocking up on these items will keep you armed for all kinds of dishes, whether it's rich and earthy, or light and fragrant.

Acid

Acid is important because it balances the richer flavours of a dish. If you have too much heavy, earthy flavour in a meal it can lead to palate fatigue, which is that feeling of heaviness or stuffiness when eating. Acid keeps your taste buds on their toes!

- Citrus fruits (lemons, limes, oranges)
- Worcestershire sauce
- Balsamic vinegar
- Rice wine
- Soy Sauce

Sweetness

This is ideal for adding an extra dimension to meat and vegetables. A bit of sweetness also brings that irresistible rich and sticky texture.

- Hoisin sauce
- Balsamic glaze
- Honey

Fat

It is essential for even cooking, for a creamy flavour, and a silky texture. I only use natural fats and avoid any artificial spreads, like margarine.

- Butter
- Extra virgin olive oil
- Rapeseed oil
- Sesame oil
- Coconut milk
- Hard cheese (parmesan, mature cheddar)

Fragrance

My spice rack is vast and my herbs are aplenty, but these are my favourites for singing aroma and flavour into a meal. Remember, whether you want to infuse zingy or earthy vibes into your dish, use fresh ingredients wherever possible.

- Garlic
- Coriander
- Ginger
- Rosemary
- Thyme
- Smoked paprika

NOTES

Right! Before we get cooking here's a few notes about the format of my recipes...

Seasoning

Salt and pepper is of course the simple foundation to help make the flavour in your food sing. I won't list salt and pepper under the ingredients nor will I always note it under the methods, because it's a given. Add these to your meals to match your personal taste. Season to your heart's content!

Serving Numbers

In my house I cook for my husband Alex and I. I've tried to be inclusive of different household sizes and I've tried not to cater solely for two or four servings, as is the norm in some recipe books. The good news is that you can simply double up or halve ingredients as required, to suit your particular household. Quite often I cook in bulk, and in this way I enjoy a couple of meals from one cooking session!

Oven Temperatures

All temperatures stated are intended for use with a fan oven. If your oven is not fan assisted, please add 20c to the temperature setting.

Measurements

The joy of cooking is that you can be spontaneous and creative. You will notice that I sometimes use general terms such as 'a handful' instead of giving a fixed measurement. In these instances you can use your intuition. This is what cooking is all about! If you fancy a big ol' handful of an ingredient, go wild, and vice versa. Enjoy the creativity and being in charge of your own taste.

I will say; the same does not apply to baking. Baking is much more of a science and you'll need to be more exact with measurements for these recipes!

Okay, let's cook!

You could be bad.

Have we got that out of the way? - Excellent.
Your first bake could be bad.
Your first stew could be bad.

Even when you're an experienced cook,
you will make mistakes.

And when you have an idea to try
something new, guess what?

It could suck.

But it could be incredible.

The person who never made a mistake,
never made anything. There is no place
for fear in the kitchen.

FOOD DIARIES: Scotland

'The mountains are calling and I must go.'

Oh Scotland, you stir something in my soul that I am so emotionally connected to. I have always felt most at home in colder weather and dramatic landscapes.

Perhaps it stems back to my favourite childhood book, 'The Hobbit'. I always identified with that idyllic, food-centric, cosy world... punctuated with the odd adventure away from comfort zones. Of course with the world of hobbits comes rustic, hearty food in abundance.

Yes, I'm sure that played a strong part in the appeal! I like to think of myself as a modern day hobbit, the way I am drawn to slow living with crackling fires, soft environments, and thick, rustic architecture - and y'know... my next meal.

My mum is Welsh, and my dad is Northern Irish, but half of my family lives in Scotland. I find as many excuses as I can to bundle my scarves and hiking boots into the car and drive up to visit whenever possible.

My perfect day in Scotland is one spent hiking high into the mountains and absorbing that breathtaking scenery - stopping for a victory picnic at the summit of course. My perfect day continues with trekking back home, weather beaten and hungry. After a hot shower and a fresh pair of fluffy socks it's settling down by the fire with red wine, before finally tucking into a comforting hot meal of meat and potatoes. Throw in some loved ones to enjoy it with and this is my own personal slice of heaven!

The best thing about these kind of days is that they're totally accessible and not once in a lifetime experiences. If wealth is measured in happiness, then I am truly rich with countless memories like these.

Simple pleasures are so important.

FOOD DIARIES: *Scotland*

FOOD DIARIES: *Scotland*

STEWS

Jo's Signature Lamb Stew with Sage Dumplings

Prep time: 35 mins   **Cooking time: 55 mins**   **Serves: 4-6**

This is a personal favourite. I created this recipe many years ago, and it will be the one that I pass down through generations. This dish fills me with complete joy. The meat is tender, the sauce is sweet and earthy, and let's not forget those delicious, comforting sage dumplings. The moment the seasons change and it becomes darker and colder outdoors, this is my go-to recipe. Enjoy!

Equipment

- bowl
- knife
- chopping board
- garlic press
- large Dutch oven or pot with a lid.
- wooden spoon

Ingredients

For the dumplings:

- 250g self raising flour
- 120g cold butter, cubed
- handful of fresh sage leaves, finely chopped

For the stew:

- knob of salted butter
- a few sprigs of fresh thyme, finely chopped
- 1 large white onion, diced
- 1 tbsp balsamic vinegar
- 3 garlic cloves, minced
- 4-6 lamb chops (bone on)
- 1/2 tube tomato puree
- 1 tbsp wholegrain mustard
- 1 courgette, thickly diced
- large handful of fresh plum tomatoes, halved
- 1 tin chopped tomatoes

Method

Preheat your oven to 180c.

First get the dumplings ready:

In a bowl rub together the flour and butter until you have a crumb-like mixture. Mix in the chopped sage and season well. Add cold water, one tablespoon at a time, and mix until a thick dough forms. Note that you won't need much water! Set aside and turn your attention to stew making...

Melt your butter with seasoning and thyme, in a large pot, on medium heat. Once heated add the diced onion and cook until soft. Add the balsamic to deglaze the pan and make the onions sweet. Add the minced garlic. Place in the lamb chops and allow them to brown on each side. Now add in the tomato purée and mustard. Stir until coated. Add the courgette, fresh tomatoes, and tinned chopped tomatoes. Stir well but carefully, so as not to break the meat. Allow to cook until the liquid has reduced and thickened.

Roll the dumpling dough into 8-10 large, thick ovals, and place in a ring around the edge of the stew. Give them a gentle press, so half of the dumpling sits in the sauce. Now cover with a lid and cook in the oven for 15 minutes. Remove the lid and bake for a further 5-10 minutes, until the dumplings are lightly golden and crisp on top.

I recommend serving with rice to soak up all that lovely tomato sauce.

Tip

If you're entertaining with this dish, make the stew the night before. The flavours will develop overnight and it'll taste even more amazing the next day. Simply bring the stew to room temperature, then top with dumplings the day of serving and cook for 15-20 minutes, uncovered at 180c.

Creamy Chicken and Smoked Bacon Stew with Cheesy Mash

Prep time: 10 mins   Cooking time: 35 mins   Serves: 6

This is the kind of dinner you make after a cold day that chilled you to the bones. The flavours in this one-pot delight are made up of familiar favourites. I always imagine eating this meal by candlelight.

Equipment

- large pot
- colander
- large Dutch oven pot
- knife
- chopping board
- garlic press
- wooden spoon
- measuring jug
- box grater
- potato masher

Ingredients

For the stew:

- 1 large white onion, diced
- 4 cloves of garlic, minced
- 2 tbsp Worcestershire sauce
- 4 chicken breasts, diced
- handful fresh thyme, finely chopped
- 2 tsp dried mixed herbs
- 200g smoked bacon lardons
- large handful of asparagus, cut into inch-long pieces
- 1 cup peas (fresh or frozen)
- 1.5 tbsp plain flour
- 200ml chicken stock
- 300ml creme fraiche

For the mash topping:

- 6 medium-large Maris Piper potatoes, cut into inch-chunks (skins on)
- 1 tbsp butter
- 100g extra strong cheddar, grated

Method

Preheat your oven to 200c. Add the potatoes to a pot of boiling water and allow it to cook for around 10-12 minutes or until soft, while you make the stew.

Add the pot to the hob on medium heat, and warm a little oil. Add the diced onions and allow it to soften for a few minutes, before adding the garlic and Worcestershire sauce. Cook for another 1-2 minutes until caramelised and golden brown.

Add the chicken breast and season generously. Stir continuously for a few minutes to cook the outside of the chicken evenly. Add the chopped thyme, mixed herbs, and bacon lardons. Stir for another 2-3 minutes then add the asparagus and peas. Add in the flour and stir well before adding the chicken stock. Allow to cook together for a further 5 minutes, before adding the creme fraiche. Stir well and reduce the heat to the lowest setting.

Now it's time to focus on the mash.

Drain the water from your potatoes and return to the pot it cooked in. Season generously, add butter and get to mashing. Once smooth, add your grated cheddar and mash once more. Remove the stew from heat and spoon mash on top. Once evenly covered, use a fork to create texture in the potato. This is how you get those delicious crispy bits. Add a little more grated cheese if desired (I mean why not), and cook pot (without lid) in the oven for 15 minutes.

Chipolata and Mushroom Stew with Mustard Mash

Prep time: 10 mins   Cooking time: 30 mins   Serves: 4

If you're looking for a mid-week comfort, or an easy weekend meal, either way this is a great staple for hearty home cooking. It gives a nod to good ol' sausage and mash then throws in a little extra pizzazz!

Equipment

- frying pan
- knife
- chopping board
- garlic Press
- 2 large pots
- wooden spoon
- measuring jug
- peeler
- colander
- potato masher

Ingredients

For the stew:

- 12 chipolatas
- 1 red onion, diced
- 4 garlic cloves, minced
- 1 pack of shiitake mushrooms, sliced
- handful of fresh rosemary, chopped
- 1 tbsp Worcestershire sauce
- 1 cup frozen peas
- 2 tbsp plain flour
- 200ml chicken stock
- 200ml milk

For the mash:

- 4-5 large Maris Piper potatoes
- 1 large knob of butter
- 1 tbsp wholegrain mustard

Method

In a frying pan, fry your chipolatas on medium heat with a little oil, until nicely browned. Once cooked remove from heat and set aside.

In a large pot, heat up some rapeseed oil and add the red onion. Once softened add the garlic, mushrooms, and rosemary. Once the mushrooms are softened, add the Worcestershire sauce and peas. When the peas soften, stir in flour a little at a time until all the ingredients are evenly coated and very thick. Now add chicken stock a little at a time, and keep stirring. Next, slowly add the milk and a delicious creamy sauce will form.

Simmer on low heat until the mixture is reduced to a rich and thick sauce. Add chipolatas to the stew and heat through once more.

Peel and dice potatoes into 2 inch thick chunks and boil for 10 minutes. Mash with butter and mustard, and season well.

Oxtail and Beef Shin Stew with Potato Gratin

Prep time: 10 mins   Cooking time: 3 hrs 30 mins   Serves: 6

This here's a one pot glory! I just love how indulgent this recipe is. It comes through in the different choices of meats, and the rich cheesy topping gives me a medieval feel when I'm cooking it! It's a recipe you can enjoy making on a relaxing afternoon with time to spare. The reward is meltingly tender meat, in a rich red wine sauce, topped with delicious potato gratin. Even better there's minimal washing up!

Equipment

- knife
- chopping board
- garlic Press
- large Dutch oven pot with a lid
- wooden spoon
- peeler
- pot
- colander

Ingredients

For the stew:

- 3 oxtail portions
- 3 beef shin portions
- 1 red onion, diced
- 2 large carrots, sliced into thick half-moons
- 3 garlic cloves, minced
- 1 tbsp oregano
- handful fresh thyme, chopped
- 2 large glasses red wine
- 3 tbsp tomato puree
- 1 tin chopped tomatoes
- 300ml beef stock

For the potato topping:

- 1kg Maris Piper potatoes, peeled and sliced
- 5 garlic cloves, minced
- 60g extra mature cheddar
- 350ml double cream

Method

Pre-heat your oven to 140c. In a large pot, heat some rapeseed oil and brown the meat on all sides for about 2 minutes. Remove from heat and set aside.

Add onions to the pot and cook in oil and meat juices until soft. Add carrots, garlic, oregano, and thyme. Cook for a minute, stirring well to combine the flavours. Add the red wine, tomato puree, chopped tomatoes, and beef stock. Allow to simmer for 10 minutes to reduce, then add the meat to the pot again, ensuring it is fully covered with the liquid.

Cover the pot with a lid and place in the oven for 2 hours 15 minutes. While this is cooking, prepare your potatoes by peeling and cutting them into thick ¾ cm slices (widthways). Parboil until tender and drain. Allow them to cool completely, until you can handle them.

When ready, remove the stew from the oven and arrange potatoes on top so that they overlap each other slightly. Once a layer is completed, sprinkle the layer with a generous amount of cheese, minced garlic, and seasoning. Repeat this process until all potatoes are added and ensure the top layer is well covered with cheese. Pour the cream over the potatoes evenly and return to the oven with no lid for 45 minutes.

I love to serve this stew in a dish with some steamed greens.

Three Bean Stew with Cheesy Potato Croquettes

Prep time: 50 mins   Cooking time: 30 mins   Serves: 4

This is a delicious, light stew that's still every bit as hearty as you'd want it to be. I love the contrast of textures within the dish: the crunch of cheesy potato croquette with the rich creaminess of the beans. Every bite is a joy! The croquettes need a little prep work but the good news is that this can be done in advance, so you can break up the cooking process if you like.

Equipment

- large pot
- colander
- potato masher
- 3x dishes
- baking tray
- knife
- peeler
- garlic Press
- chopping board
- large frying pan
- wooden spoon

Ingredients

For the croquettes:

- 3 large Maris Piper potatoes
- 1.5 tsp smoked paprika
- 1 tbsp mixed herbs
- handful fresh chives, chopped
- 120g extra mature cheddar, grated
- 100g plain flour
- 2 eggs
- 100g panko breadcrumbs

For the stew:

- 1 large red onion, diced
- 3 garlic cloves, minced
- 1 tbsp balsamic vinegar
- 2 large carrots, peeled, quartered, and finely sliced
- handful fresh thyme, chopped
- 3 tbsp tomato puree

Method

Begin by preparing potato croquettes:

Dice potatoes into inch sized pieces (no need to peel them), and boil until fully cooked. Drain and mash, adding in the smoked paprika, mixed herbs, chives, and grated cheese. Mix well, and put mash in the fridge to chill for 30 minutes. This will make it easier to form into croquettes.

Once chilled, take heaped tablespoonfuls of mash, and using clean hands, form into inch thick cylinders. You should get 12 croquettes from your batch.

Preheat your oven to 200c.

Place flour, 2 beaten eggs, and panko breadcrumbs in three separate dishes, respectively. Take each croquette and coat in the flour, then egg, and then a generous coating of panko, and place onto a baking tray. Once all of your croquettes are formed, place in the oven for 30 minutes.

Now it's time to make the stew:

In a large frying pan on medium-low heat, add red onion and garlic, and once softened, deglaze the pan with balsamic vinegar. Add carrots, thyme, and tomato puree, and stir well. After a couple of minutes stir in flour, and once all ingredients are coated, add vegetable stock and Worcestershire sauce.

Allow the stock to reduce a little before adding the tomatoes and mixed beans (drained). Stir through. Allow to simmer and reduce into a delicious, thick sauce. Finish by stirring through natural yoghurt.

Serve your bean stew in a dish and top with the crispy potato croquettes.

Three Bean Stew with Cheesy Potato Croquettes

Ingredients (cont)

- 1 tbsp plain flour
- 350ml vegetable stock
- 1 tbsp Worcestershire sauce
- 2 handfuls of plum tomatoes, halved
- 1 tin mixed beans
- 2 tbsp natural yoghurt

Tip

Unlike regular mash, don't be tempted to add butter or milk to the potatoes. This will make the mash too soft to form croquettes.

FOOD DIARIES: *Japan*

I've always viewed Japan with total wonder, because of the marvellous clash between past and present! It hit me more than ever in Akasaka, where I sat drinking beer outside a tiny, ancient stone building, towered over by a huge, gleaming skyscraper, which was located directly next door. It was a surreal moment. Alex and I dreamt of visiting Japan since we first became a couple in 2005, and when we finally took the trip in 2019, it really felt like our long awaited food pilgrimage.

We spent two weeks there, trying to experience as much as we possibly could in the time we had. There is so much to see and do in Japan. We ate ramen in Shibuya, gyoza in Harajuku, sushi in Dotonbori, and drank far too much beer in Kyoto.

One of our favourite days was the day we visited an old school friend of Alex's. His friend moved back to Japan some twenty years ago, and we hired bikes and cycled all over Kyoto. We ended up going to places that we as tourists, could never have sought out ourselves. I remember feeling like I was in a computer game as we cycled through the streets in convoy, beers in our bellies, the sunset lighting up the sky in orange and pink, and as dusk fell, the innumerable neon lights that are so synonymous with Japan, beginning to glow.

It was an unforgettable trip, and both the food and culture were nothing short of inspiring. What I admire most about Japanese culture is the pursuit of excellence in everything, no matter how small or seemingly simple the venture. The food is executed with such passion and pride, but without any pretentious overtones. As I watched food prepared in the many open restaurant kitchens, I admired the respectful, almost ceremonious way in which the ingredients were treated.

While our enthusiasm for Japanese cuisine can never match generations of history, our love for the food translates into our everyday cooking in the form of chewy noodles, warming broth, and crispy fried meat. Simple. Wholesome. Passionate. This is the food I love best!

FOOD DIARIES: *Japan*

FOOD DIARIES: *Japan*

NOODLES AND PASTA

Creamy Chicken and Mushroom Noodle Soup

Prep time: 5 mins + 2 hours marinating   **Cooking time: 15 mins**   **Serves: 2**

Noodle soup is absolute perfection for a quick, filling meal, and it's also a great way to use up leftovers. The effort to satisfaction ratio makes this such a great dish for hearty lunches or speedy dinners.

Equipment

- bowl
- knife
- chopping board
- garlic Press
- large pot
- frying pan
- wooden spoon

Ingredients

For the chicken:

- 3 boneless chicken thighs
- 1 tbsp honey
- 1 tbsp dark soy
- 1 tbsp light soy
- 1 tbsp rice wine

For the noodle broth:

- small white onion, sliced
- 2 garlic cloves, minced
- large handful wild mushrooms, sliced
- 1 tbsp dark soy
- 1 tbsp light soy
- 1 tbsp rice wine
- 500ml chicken stock (page 115)
- quarter can coconut milk
- 120g egg noodles

For garnish:

- 2 spring onions, finely chopped
- sesame seeds
- 2 tsp chilli crisp oil

Method

Begin by marinating the chicken thighs. In a bowl, add the chicken, honey, dark soy, light soy, and rice wine. Mix well and marinate for 2 hours.

In a pot, fry the onions and garlic in a little oil (sesame oil is ideal for flavour), on medium heat until softened. Then add the sliced mushrooms and fry for a few more minutes. Now add the dark and light soy, rice wine, chicken stock, and coconut milk. Simmer for 5 minutes on low heat.

Add in the egg noodles. Allow to cook until softened. While the noodles are cooking, fry the chicken thighs in a frying pan on low-medium heat, for about 4 minutes on each side, until cooked through.

Time to serve up! Add the noodles to serving bowls and top with broth. Slice the chicken thighs thinly, and add on top of the noodles. Garnish with spring onions, a sprinkling of sesame seeds and chilli crisp oil.

Tip

Utilise leftovers by topping this dish with cooked chicken from another meal. Simply slice cooked chicken, marinate for 1 hour, and heat through in the frying pan.

Pan Fried Sirloin with Sticky Udon Noodles

Prep time: 2 mins   **Cooking time: 10 mins**   **Serves: 2**

Noodles are a go-to speedy meal in my house. They're versatile, tasty, and filling. I love how dark these noodles turn with the rich hoisin and soy. This meal is sweet and sticky, which is lovely with a nice pink steak - and sirloin is a great cost effective, leaner option for mid-week meals.

Equipment

- knife
- chopping board
- large pot
- colander
- 2x frying pan
- wooden spoon

Ingredients

- 150g fresh Udon noodles
- 1 onion, thinly sliced
- 2 tbsp dark soy
- 2 tbsp light soy
- 1 tbsp mirin
- 1 tbsp hoisin
- 1 large sirloin steak
- sesame seeds for garnish (optional, but lovely)

Method

Begin by blanching the Udon for 2 minutes in boiling water to soften, then drain and set aside.

In a pan, on medium heat, add a little oil (sesame oil is ideal for a subtle nutty flavour) and fry the onion until softened. Add the Udon to the pan and fry together for a couple of minutes. Then add the soy, mirin, and hoisin, and cook down until dark and thick.

While this mixture is reducing, in another pan, fry the steak. Season well and add to a very hot pan with a little oil. Cook for 2 minutes on each side, for medium rare.

Add noodles to a bowl and top with thin slices of juicy steak. Drizzle with a little more hoisin and sprinkle with sesame seeds. I recommend enjoying this with a side of lovely crisp pak choi.

Sticky Honey Soy Chicken with Coconut Noodles

Prep time: 10 mins + 6 hours marinating   Cooking time: 25 mins   Serves: 2

This dish is such a treat for the tastebuds! There is quite a process to this dish but the reward is delicious, sweet and sticky chicken pieces, served with rich, creamy noodles. It's a fantastic alternative to takeaway, and the flavours will blow your mind!

Equipment

- knife
- chopping board
- garlic press
- 2x large bowls
- 2x frying pan
- 3x wooden spoon
- wire rack
- pot
- colander

Ingredients

For the honey soy chicken:

- 2 large chicken breasts, diced into inch-sized chunks
- 1 tbsp light soy sauce
- 1 tbsp dark soy sauce
- 1 tbsp honey
- 100g plain flour
- vegetable oil for deep frying

For the coconut noodles:

- 4 nests of dried egg noodles
- 1 onion, sliced
- 2 garlic cloves, minced
- 1 tbsp dark soy sauce
- 1 tbsp light soy sauce
- 1 tbsp thai red curry paste
- 200ml coconut milk

For the sticky chicken sauce:

- 1 tbsp sesame oil
- 1 onion, sliced
- 3 garlic cloves, minced

Method

First, let's prepare the honey soy chicken. This ideally starts with a marinade made the night before, for maximum flavour. At a minimum, prepare the marinade 6 hours before cooking. Take diced chicken and add to a bowl with the dark soy, light soy, and honey. Stir well to coat the chicken evenly then cover and refrigerate.

When the marinade has been made and left to work its magic, it's time to cook. Remove the chicken from the fridge and prepare the coating. In a large, separate bowl, add the plain flour and season liberally with salt and pepper. Now add the chicken and carefully stir or toss to evenly coat all pieces.

Half fill a deep, heavy pan with vegetable oil and heat to 175c. Once up to temperature, carefully add small batches of coated chicken (around 6 pieces) and fry until rich, golden brown. This should take around 4 minutes. Be sure to flip any pieces which are not cooking evenly in the oil.

Remove the cooked chicken and place on a wire rack to cool. Remember not to crowd the rack, or the lovely, crispy chicken will go soggy! Repeat this process until all the chicken is cooked.

Next we'll make the coconut noodles. Add the noodle nests to salted, boiling water until softened, but not fully cooked. This should take around 3-4 minutes. Drain and rinse with cool water to stop the cooking process.

In a large frying pan or wok, fry the onion and garlic in sesame oil over medium to high heat, for 2 minutes. Next, add the dark and light soy, and red thai curry paste. Stir, while cooking for 2 minutes. Now add coconut milk to the pan and lower the heat, bringing to a low simmer, before adding the semi-cooked noodles.

Sticky Honey Soy Chicken with Coconut Noodles

Ingredients (cont)

For the sticky chicken sauce:

- 1 tbsp light soy sauce
- 1 tbsp dark soy sauce
- 1 tbsp honey
- 1 tbsp oyster sauce
- 1 tbsp rice wine

Gently stir over low heat until noodles are cooked through and absorb the coconut milk. This should take around 5 minutes.

Now it's time to make that glorious, sweet and sticky sauce. In a frying pan add the sesame oil, garlic, and sliced onions. Fry on high heat for 2 minutes. Once the onion has softened, add the dark soy, light soy, and honey. Then add the oyster sauce and rice wine, continually stirring until the mixture reduces and starts to thicken.

Once the sauce becomes thick and sticky (you can add some corn flour if you like to speed up the process), add the crispy fried chicken to the pan, and carefully fold into the sauce.

Serve in bowls or deep dishes, starting with a bed of creamy coconut noodles topped with the freshly coated, sticky, crispy chicken. Garnish with chopped spring onions and sesame seeds, if desired.

A GUIDE TO MAKING PASTA

Homemade pasta sounds incredibly impressive and perhaps a little daunting, but I promise you that it's straightforward and most of all – fun!

Pasta making can come with a lot of bells and whistles (the daunting bit!) Ultimately these do give you the best and most authentic final product, but I really feel that not having the perfect gadgets shouldn't scare you away from making food from scratch. So I'm going to run through the options for making your own pasta at home. I've tried all methods on my own journey.

Ideal	Perfectly Fine
00 flour: milled for a finer texture, which makes pasta silky, but not always easy to find in shops.	Plain flour: your pasta will still be delicious.
Pasta machine: makes rolling dough to the desired thickness and shape a breeze, but they can be pricey.	Rolling pin: if you don't mind some good old fashioned elbow grease then you can roll pasta dough by hand.
Ravioli stamp: a cheap tool that makes your ravioli uniform and quick to process.	Knife and fork: Simply cut your ravioli to size and seal the edges with a fork.

Making the dough

This bit is easy. All you need is a weighing scale and a fork. Pasta is made of only flour and eggs. There are many different opinions on ratios, and after experimenting, my preference is 90g flour and 1 egg, per portion of pasta.

Make a well in the middle of the flour (you can do this in a bowl to keep things clean and contained), and crack the eggs into the centre. Using the fork; beat the egg and begin to pull in flour from the outside to combine. Keep doing this until a thick paste forms. Once it is too thick for the fork, use your hands to combine the rest of the flour into dough.

On a clean surface, knead the dough for 5 minutes until it is smooth and springs back when poked. Wrap in cling film and chill for 20 minutes.

Rolling the dough

Cut the chilled dough into halves or quarters, depending on how much you are making. This will make it manageable to process. Keep the rest wrapped in cling film so it doesn't dry out. When rolling your dough, always have a well floured surface and rolling pin to prevent the dough from sticking.

For pasta machines

Use a rolling pin to roll the dough into a thick oval. Pasta machines have a thickness setting on the press. When the dough runs through, it gets rolled thinner and thinner each time. The aim is for the dough to be near translucent. You should see the shadow of your fingers when placed behind the dough.

A GUIDE TO MAKING PASTA

Be sure to lightly flour your sheet of dough each time it passes through, to prevent it from sticking.

If the ends of your rolls of pasta sheets are tapered or if you get a tear, simply fold the ends of the sheet over and pass it through the machine. You can do this until you have a uniform sheet of pasta.

For rolling by hand

Ensure that your rolling pin is generously floured to prevent sticking.

Once the pasta gets to a certain degree of thinness, I recommend using one hand to hold the dough while rolling with the other hand. This encourages the dough to stretch, rather than bounce back. Rolling by hand is hard work, but it can be done - I believe in you!

Spinach Ravioli with Lemon and Sage Butter

Prep time: 30 mins + 20 mins chilling   Cooking time: 3 mins   Serves: 2

Once I learned how to make my own pasta I was hooked. Ravioli is one of my favourite pastas, and in my opinion, absolutely the most fun to make. What could be more joyful than little squishy food parcels?! I think this is a great dish for those starting out in pasta making. It'll have you hooked on homemade in no time.

Equipment

- weighing scales
- fork
- pasta machine
- ravioli stamp
- large bowl
- teaspoon
- baking tray
- large pot
- small saucepan
- slotted spoon

Ingredients

For the pasta:

- 180g 00 flour
- 2 eggs

For the filling:

- 1 large handful spinach, finely chopped
- 2 garlic cloves, minced
- 125g mascarpone
- 50g parmesan
- ½ tsp ground nutmeg

For the sauce:

- juice of half a lemon
- 3 tbsp butter
- 6 sage leaves, finely chopped

Method

Add flour to a clean, dry surface and create a well in the centre. Crack eggs into the middle of the flour (the well), and use a fork to beat the eggs, combining flour from the edges as you go. Slowly, you will build up a paste. Once it becomes very thick, set aside the fork, and using clean hands, gather flour into the centre of the egg mix. Combine until you have a ball of dough. Knead this for 5 minutes until it is smooth and springs back to the touch. Wrap in cling film and refrigerate for 20 minutes, while making the filling.

In a large bowl, add chopped spinach, garlic, mascarpone, parmesan, and nutmeg. Stir until evenly combined.

Pasta making time!

Once chilled, cut the dough into two pieces so it is easier to work with. Roll pasta (see page 39), until it is thin and translucent. It should be about a handspan wide.

Lay the length of pasta out on a floured surface and place small teaspoonfuls of the spinach mixture at two finger intervals. Fold your pasta sheet in half, over the top of the mixture. Starting at one end and working your way down, use your fingers to shape around the filling, squeezing out any air, sealing the ravioli. Use a ravioli stamp to press out the pasta shapes, or use a knife to cut the ravioli squares and seal the edges with a fork.

Place the completed pasta onto a baking tray dusted with flour. Place them filling side down to prevent drying out. Repeat the process with the other half of the pasta.

Add the ravioli to boiling, salted water and cook for 3 minutes. While this is cooking, add butter, lemon juice, and sage to a saucepan. Cook on medium-low heat until melted and combined.

Spinach Ravioli with Lemon and Sage Butter

Remove the pasta from the water with a slotted spoon (ravioli deserves a gentle touch!) and serve in dishes with the lovely lemon butter sauce spooned over the top. Finish with black pepper and a fresh grating of parmesan.

Tip

Go easy with filling up the pasta. Too much, and the ravioli will burst when cooking! Aim to fill each centre with two thirds of a teaspoon.

Zingy Lemon Fusilli with Wilted Greens

Prep time: 5 mins   **Cooking time: 15 mins**   **Serves: 2**

This dish is quick and easy and delivers big on flavour. It makes a tasty and fresh meal for lunch or dinner, when hunger just won't wait.

Equipment

- 2x pot
- knife
- chopping board
- garlic press
- frying pan
- wooden spoon
- colander

Ingredients

- 150g fusilli pasta
- handful tenderstem broccoli, sliced into 1 inch pieces
- 1 tbsp salted butter
- 1 white onion, finely sliced into strips
- 2 tbsp balsamic vinegar
- 1 vegetable stock cube
- 4 garlic cloves, minced
- half pack cherry tomatoes, halved
- 2 tbsp red pesto
- 1 bag rocket
- 1 bunch flat leaf parsley, chopped
- zest of 1 lemon

Method

Add the pasta to a large pot of boiling, salted water and cook until al dente. In a separate pot, cook the broccoli in boiling water, covering with water three-quarter way up. Cook for 3 minutes until tender but with a little bite. No soggy vegetables here!

In a pan, melt butter on medium heat. Add the onions and once softened, stir in the balsamic vinegar. Stir in stock cube and garlic. Add the drained broccoli pieces and tomatoes to the pan and stir through.

Once the pasta is cooked, drain and return to the pot, and stir in the pesto. Add the rocket, which will begin to wilt from the heat of the pasta. Finally, right before serving, stir in fresh, chopped parsley and lemon zest.

Tip

White truffle oil. That's it. I recommend investing in some, and use it sparingly. Watch your pasta take on a whole new dimension. I am obsessed with this stuff.

Pea and Smoked Bacon Spaghetti

Prep time: 5 mins   Cooking time: 15 mins   Serves: 2

Ah, peas and bacon... best friends! In my household this is affectionately known as 'green pasta'. It is a lovely fresh twist on the classic carbonara, and of course we have to talk about that incredible colour!

Equipment

- large pot
- frying pan
- wooden spoon
- food processor
- colander

Ingredients

- 120g spaghetti
- 100g smoked bacon lardons
- 200g peas
- large bunch fresh basil
- 2 tbsp olive oil
- 2 garlic cloves
- 2 tbsp creme fraiche
- 20g parmesan
- zest of 1 lemon

Method

Add spaghetti to a large pot with boiling water and leave to cook until al-dente.

While the spaghetti is cooking, heat the frying pan on medium heat, and cook the bacon lardons for 5 minutes. They don't need oil as they are fatty enough.

In a food processor, add peas, basil, olive oil, and garlic cloves. Season well. Blend until it makes a smooth paste, and take a moment to enjoy that glorious green!

Add the pea and basil paste to the pan. Now add the creme fraiche and stir on low heat to warm through. By now your pasta should be cooked. Drain it, and add to the frying pan immediately. Stir, to mix the sauce into the pasta evenly.

Grate in the parmesan and add the lemon zest, also adding 1 tbsp of lemon juice. Finish with another grating of parmesan on top and a drizzle of extra virgin olive oil.

Tip

It is absolutely fine to use either fresh or frozen peas. If using frozen peas, do make sure they are thoroughly thawed before use. Place peas in a bowl and pour boiling water over it. Drain after one minute, for tender peas.

Mac and Cheese with Caramelised Onion and Bacon Crumb

Prep time: 20 mins   Cooking time: 20 mins   Serves: 4

You don't need me to tell you that Mac and Cheese is like a hug in a bowl - a big, cheesy, filthy hug. This version is packed with earthy, herby flavours, and topped with spicy sweet onion, and a crunchy smoked bacon crumb. You're guaranteed to love this adaptation of an incredibly comforting dish.

Equipment

- chopping board
- knife
- garlic press
- frying pan
- 2 large pots
- colander
- whisk

Ingredients

For the caramelised onion:

- 2 tbsp butter
- 1 large white onion, finely sliced
- 1 tbsp balsamic vinegar
- 2 tbsp chilli jam

For the breadcrumb topping:

- 100g smoked bacon lardons
- 50g panko breadcrumbs
- 3 tbsp pumpkin seeds

For the Mac and Cheese:

- 300g penne pasta
- 30g butter
- 2 tbsp plain flour
- 300ml milk
- 4 garlic cloves, minced
- 1 tsp mixed herbs
- 1 handful fresh rosemary, finely chopped
- 100g extra mature cheddar, grated
- 80g Gruyere, grated

Method

First, let's get started on those sweet caramelised onions. In a frying pan, on low-medium heat, add butter. Once melted, add the sliced onions and fry until soft. Now add the balsamic vinegar and fry for 2 minutes until nice and dark. Then add chilli jam. Reduce to a low heat and stir regularly for 5-10 minutes, until the onions are very soft, translucent, and sticky looking. Remove from heat and set aside.

In a clean frying pan (give the one you just used a rinse - efficiency and all that), fry the bacon lardons on medium heat, until crispy. Now add the breadcrumbs and pumpkin seeds. Season well, and toast. You can add a little olive oil to assist with toasting. Remove from heat and set aside when the breadcrumbs are rich golden brown.

Okay it's Mac and Cheese time!

Boil your penne pasta until al dente. Drain and set aside.

In a large pot, on low-medium heat, melt the butter and add flour. Whisk together until a paste forms. Slowly add the milk, and keep whisking until the mixture is fully combined and smooth. Add garlic, mixed herbs, and rosemary. Now add the grated cheddar and Gruyere. Stir continuously until the cheese melts and combines together to create a deliciously thick cheese sauce.

Add the cooked and drained penne pasta to the sauce, and mix well. Serve, and top with caramelised onion, and a generous sprinkling of bacon crumb.

Tip

Love classic macaroni? Go for it! I personally love the bigger tubes of penne, but you can use whatever pasta you like of course.

'Have nothing in your houses that you do not know to be useful or believe to be beautiful.'

— William Morris.

This is one of my favourite quotes. It works wonders for creating a mindful living space.

I apply a similar mantra to the way I eat. Nothing passes my lips that will not nourish either my body or my soul, in that moment.

I listen out for which I need most.

My body needs fresh, nutritious ingredients.

And sometimes my soul needs cheesecake.

FOOD DIARIES: *Guyana*

I was seventeen when I first ate Guyanese food. It was love at first bite. I'm talking eye-rollingly good. It instantly skyrocketed its way to become one of my favourite genres of food on the planet. The flavours are so rich and complex. It's earthy and herby with plenty of bay and thyme, but it's also sweet and fragrant, with infusions of cinnamon and Cassareep. Cassareep is a sweet syrup made from the cassava root. It's extremely hard to get hold of over here and will only grow in certain soil. It isn't cultivated in the UK. I love hearing the lengths that Alex's family goes to just to be able to cook with it!

Guyana is located just above Brazil, making it geographically South American, but culturally it is connected with the Caribbean. I've heard so many fun stories from family members about their childhoods, about the parties that lasted until 6am (and who could drink the most rum), and the breathtaking excursions into the Amazon interior. I've also heard wild accounts of a ghost in Alex's grandad's home who roams the guest wing. I've a good mind to introduce myself to him one day!

The absolute best kind of people for me, are people who love to eat, and wow, do Alex's family love to eat! Just writing about the spreads that get served at gatherings has me excited! Over the years aunties have shown me tips and tricks for recreating Guyanese food, but I honestly cannot compare. I watch over their shoulders for the authentic experience like an excited child waiting for presents at Christmas. Influences do find their way into our cooking, most commonly seen with sticky coconut rice and fragrant curries.

RICE

Tamarind Duck with Rice

Prep time: 5 mins   **Cooking time: 20 mins**   **Serves: 2**

This is a happy, zingy dish full of fresh flavour! Tamarind has an incredible sweet and sour taste, and when teamed with the richness of duck, it makes such a formidable combination. This is the kind of meal that will make you do a happy dance on the first bite!

Equipment

- kitchen towel
- chopping board
- garlic press
- very sharp knife
- large frying pan
- wooden Spoon
- zester

Ingredients

- 2 duck breasts
- 1 large red onion, sliced
- 4 garlic cloves, minced
- 130g baby sweetcorn, sliced
- 150g tenderstem broccoli, sliced
- 1 tbsp honey
- 5 tbsp tamarind sauce
- 1 inch fresh ginger, grated
- 1.5 tsp turmeric
- half tin coconut milk
- handful coriander, chopped

Method

First prep the duck by patting the skin dry with a kitchen towel, then use a very sharp knife to score diagonal cuts into the skin, 5mm apart. Rub plenty of salt into the skin.

Heat the pan on medium. Once hot, add the duck, skin side down. No oil is needed as the duck fat will render down very quickly. Spoon off any fat released from the skin while cooking (but don't throw it away). This will keep the skin crispy.

After 5 minutes, or when the skin is browned and crispy, flip the duck and cook the meat on low-medium, for 5 minutes. Remove the duck and set aside.

Keep the pan on low-medium heat and return a little of the duck fat that you drained, then add the onions and garlic. Once softened, add the sweetcorn and broccoli. Stir-fry for a few minutes, before adding the honey, tamarind sauce, ginger, turmeric, and coconut milk.

When the veggies are tender, thinly slice the duck and return to the pan. Once heated through, stir in the coriander and serve immediately with basmati rice.

Tip

Tamarind sauces can vary in potency. Some may be very tart, while others are a little sweeter. Try adding a few tablespoons first, then tasting to see if you prefer the full 5 that I recommend.

Mushroom and Thyme Coconut Rice

Prep time: 5 mins   **Cooking time: 20 mins**   **Serves: 4**

Sticky coconut rice is an absolute favourite in my house. For me, sticky rice beats fluffy rice any day. It feels so much more hearty and comforting. This coconut rice is packed with rich textures and flavour, making it a punchy side dish, or bold enough to stand as a meal on its own.

Equipment

- chopping board
- knife
- garlic press
- medium pot
- wooden spoon
- kettle

Ingredients

- 1 large red onion, diced
- 4 garlic cloves, minced
- 250g chestnut mushrooms, sliced
- 200g basmati rice
- 2 tsp mixed herbs
- 2 chicken stock cubes
- 1 handful fresh thyme, chopped
- 1 tin coconut milk

Method

Heat a little rapeseed oil in a pot, on medium heat, and add onions. Cook for 2-3 minutes until softened, then the add garlic and sliced mushrooms.

Allow the mushrooms to cook for a minute. Add the rice, mixed herbs, and stock cubes. Cook it dry for a minute or so, allowing the concentrated flavour of the stock cubes to break down and infuse into the rice. Now cover the rice about 1cm above the top, with boiling water. Stir well until the stock cubes are dissolved.

When the liquid reduces to the level of the rice, add the chopped thyme and coconut milk. Stir frequently to prevent the rice from sticking to the bottom of the pan. As the milk cooks down, the rice will become thick. The dish is complete when there is no liquid left, and the rice is lovely and sticky.

Tomato and Smoked Paprika Coconut Rice

Prep time: 5 mins   Cooking time: 20 mins   Serves: 4

The colour of this dish is glorious. It finishes in a wonderful crimson red that'll brighten up any plate! I think coconut rice is synonymous with comfort food, and the rich and creamy texture is given real depth with a hit of smoked paprika. This dish pairs incredibly well with lamb chops or a lovely steak.

Equipment

- knife
- chopping board
- garlic press
- medium pot
- wooden spoon
- kettle

Ingredients

- 1 large red onion, diced
- 4 garlic cloves, minced
- 1 tsp mixed herbs
- 1.5 tsp smoked paprika
- 2 tbsp tomato puree
- 1 tsp Worcestershire sauce
- 2 vegetable stock cubes
- 200g basmati rice
- half a pack of plum tomatoes, halved
- 1 tin of sweetcorn
- 1 handful fresh thyme, chopped
- 1 tin coconut milk

Method

Add some rapeseed oil to a pot on medium heat, and cook the onions and garlic together until the onions soften. Now add the mixed herbs, smoked paprika, tomato puree, Worcestershire sauce, and vegetable stock cubes. Mix well.

Add basmati rice and cook dry for a minute or two, allowing the flavours to infuse into the rice. Then add boiling water, covering the rice about 1cm above the top. When the liquid reduces to the level of the rice, add the tomatoes, sweetcorn, thyme, and coconut milk.

Cook for 15-20 minutes stirring regularly, until the coconut milk has reduced right down and the rice is creamy and sticky.

Alex's Famous Chicken Katsu

Prep time: 15 mins   **Cooking time: 30 mins**   **Serves: 4**

Of all the Japanese cuisine that we love, my husband's favourite dish is Chicken Katsu. So much so, he was determined to learn how to make it himself, so that we could enjoy it at home whenever we pleased. After a lot of trial, Alex created his own version of the dish and it was such a success that our friends request it whenever they come over for dinner!

Equipment

- knife
- chopping board
- garlic press
- meat tenderizer or rolling pin
- 3x dishes
- 2x frying pan

Ingredients

For the chicken:

- 2 chicken breasts
- 80g plain flour
- 1 egg
- 80g panko breadcrumbs

For the katsu sauce:

- 2 tsp sesame oil
- 1 white onion, finely diced
- 1 garlic clove, minced
- 1 inch fresh ginger, grated
- 1 tbsp soy sauce
- 2 tsp mirin
- 2 tsp rice wine vinegar
- 2 blocks of Japanese curry roux
- 500ml chicken stock
- spring onions, garnish
- sesame seeds, garnish
- hoisin sauce, garnish

Method

Using a meat tenderizer or rolling pin, hammer the chicken breasts until nice and thin. Set them on a plate and in 3 separate dishes place flour, beaten egg, and panko. Season the flour.

Dip the breasts into the flour, then into the egg, and then into the panko. Be sure to get lots of breadcrumbs on there for plenty of crunch. Set aside.

In a frying pan, fry the onions in the sesame oil for a few minutes, until softened. Then add the garlic and ginger. Fry for 2 more minutes. Add the soy, mirin, and rice wine vinegar. Stir for a few more minutes. Add in the curry roux and chicken stock. Simmer on low heat while stirring occasionally for 10 minutes.

While that simmers, add the breaded chicken to a medium hot pan with 3 tbsp sesame oil. Cook for 4-5 minutes on each side, until they are gloriously crispy.

To serve, plate up a dome of rice and pour the thick katsu sauce around it. Then add the crispy chicken, sliced and topped with freshly chopped spring onions, and sesame seeds. Take this dish up a notch with a final drizzle of hoisin sauce over the chicken.

Tip

For perfect domes of rice, simply fill a small bowl with rice then flip it upside down on the plate. Very satisfying to do!

Creamy Lamb and Potato Curry

Prep time: 5 mins + 6 hours marinating   **Cooking time: 35 mins**   **Serves: 4**

Years ago I nicknamed my husband the curry king, because of the way he knocks up the most tender, delicious curries with his own personal twist. This curry is a winner year round for a dish that's rich and warming. Get ready for the most beautiful, tender lamb!

Equipment

- knife
- chopping board
- blender
- bowl
- large pot with lid
- wooden spoon
- medium pot

Ingredients

For the marinade:

- 4 lamb steaks, diced
- 3 spring onions
- 1 carrot
- juice of 1 lime
- 100g cherry tomatoes
- handful fresh coriander
- 4 garlic cloves, minced
- 1 red chilli, finely chopped

For the curry:

- 1 tbsp rapeseed oil
- 1 tbsp butter
- 1 white onion, diced
- 3 tbsp curry powder
- 4 medium white potatoes, diced with skin on
- half a can coconut milk
- coriander to garnish

Method

Place the marinade ingredients for the lamb into a blender. Blitz with 150ml water until a paste forms. Add this to a bowl with the diced lamb, and leave to marinate for 6 hours, minimum.

In a large pot, fry the diced onion in rapeseed oil and butter until soft and golden brown. Season generously and add curry powder. Now add the lamb and the marinade. Stir well, and cook on low heat with the lid on for 30 minutes.

Add the potatoes to salted, boiling water and cook for 10 minutes. Drain and set aside. Let the curry cook for 30 minutes, then add the potatoes and coconut milk. Stir through.

Serve with basmati rice, and a sprinkle of freshly chopped coriander to garnish.

Creamy Tarragon Chicken and Rice

Prep time: 10 mins   Cooking time: 20 mins   Serves: 4

I couldn't write this book without paying homage to where it all started! Yes, this is the first dish I ever learned to make, and it has seen me through my childhood, university, and is still a regular meal in my house. This meal is a simple staple, and a fantastic foundation on which you can build and experiment with other flavours.

Equipment

- chopping board
- knife
- garlic press
- large pan
- wooden spoon

Ingredients

- 1 large white onion, diced
- 2 garlic cloves, minced
- 1 tbsp balsamic vinegar
- 2 chicken breasts, diced
- 1.5 tsp mixed herbs
- pack of chestnut mushrooms, sliced
- 2 tbsp plain flour
- 500ml milk
- 1 cup of peas
- handful fresh tarragon, chopped

Method

Heat a pan on medium with a glug of rapeseed oil. Once hot, add onions. Stir regularly and cook until the onion turns translucent and light brown. Add garlic and balsamic vinegar. Cook for 2 minutes.

Next add the chicken, and season well. Add mixed herbs. Stir and cook for around 5 minutes until the chicken is cooked on all sides. Add the mushrooms and stir through until softened.

Next, sprinkle in flour, and stir until everything in the pan is well coated. It will become very thick. Start pouring in the milk, a little at a time, and stir continuously to prevent lumps. A creamy sauce will form. Reduce the heat a little and add the peas and tarragon. Cook for another 5-10 minutes until the sauce reduces, and the chicken is cooked through.

Serve with basmati rice.

"What are you cooking? That smells incredible!"

Onions and garlic... it's always just onions and garlic! So many great food stories begin with these two simple ingredients.

GROWING YOUR OWN

After spending fifteen years living in flats, there was nothing I wanted more from my first house than to grow vegetables in the garden. Don't let anyone tell you that growing your own food is always a breeze. Some plants are easier than others for sure, but nonetheless, it can take a fair amount of love and care to see your vegetables through... and a lot of fretting over the weather.

Like anything, the reward is better when you've worked for it. The effort of growing your own is absolutely worth it, just for the sheer happiness you feel when that hard earned food ends up on your plate. I have never appreciated vegetables more.

When to Sow and Harvest

Plant	Sow	Harvest
Asparagus	Jan-Feb	Apr-Jun
Broad beans	Feb-May	May-Oct
Basil	Feb-Jul	Jun-Sep
Beetroot	Mar-Jul	Jun-Oct
Broccoli	Apr-Jun	Jul-Aug
Cabbage	Feb-Jun	Jun-Oct
Carrots	Feb-Aug	Jun-Oct
Cauliflower	Jan-Jun	Jul-Nov
Celeriac	Feb-Apr	Oct-Dec
Celery	Feb-May	Jul-Nov
Cucumber	Feb-Apr	Apr-Jul
Dill	Apr-Jul	Jul-Sep
Endive	Mar-Jul	Jul-Oct
French beans	Apr-Jun	May-Oct
Garlic	Feb-Apr	Jun-Aug
Leek	Mar-May	Jul-Nov
Lettuce	Feb-Aug	Jun-Sep
Onion	Feb-Apr	Aug-Oct
Parsley	Feb-Jul	Jun-Sep
Peas	Mar-Jun	Jun-Sep
Peppers	Mar-Apr	Jun-Oct
Spinach	Mar-Jul	Apr-Oct
Squash	Mar-Apr	Jun-Sep
Strawberry	Dec-Jan	May-Sep
Tomato	Nov-Mar	Aug-Oct

If you want to experience a deep emotional connection with food, then I urge you to grow your own.

Suddenly it isn't just a tomato. It is your tomato.

It begins as a dry speck that you plant into the soil with total skepticism, and probably leave on your windowsill and forget about - until one morning... a little green shoot appears. Cue excitement and uncertainty. What next?! Water it? Leave it alone? Plant it outside? That little shoot is now your project and you worry about its needs daily.

Soon it becomes a source of pride as it blooms, and grows, and begins to sprout little green fruit. You did it - tomatoes! They blush and turn a juicy, rich red in the sun.

Finally, they are plucked and brought back to your kitchen in proud and gentle handfuls.

On your plate, homegrown vegetables have a story. Each little tomato was cared for and took months to grow into just one little morsel. You enjoy it all the more because you made it!

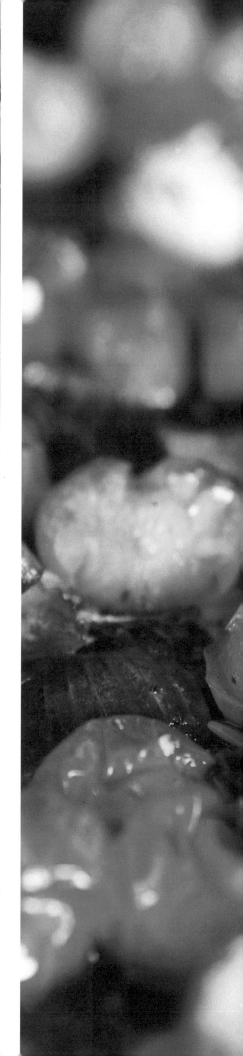

SIDES

Roasted Tomato Salsa

Prep time: 5 mins   **Cooking time: 30 mins**   **Serves: 4**

You don't ever have to buy from a jar again! A few simple ingredients and minimal effort is all you need for a delicious, versatile salsa that will liven up so many meals. It goes fantastic with chicken, fish, and is even great in sandwiches.

Equipment

- knife
- chopping board
- baking tray
- blender (optional)

Ingredients

- 2 dozen vine ripened tomatoes
- 1 red onion, diced
- 5 garlic cloves
- 2 tbsp olive oil
- 1 tbsp balsamic vinegar
- 1 tbsp mixed herbs
- 1 tsp chilli flakes
- a few sprigs of fresh thyme

Method

Preheat oven to 160c. Add tomatoes (whole), diced onion, and garlic cloves to the baking tray. Pour the olive oil and balsamic vinegar over it, and mix well. Sprinkle over the mixed herbs, chilli flakes, and thyme leaves, removed from the stem. Season generously.

Stir once more to coat all ingredients evenly. Place the tray in the oven and roast for 30 minutes. Your kitchen is going to smell incredible!

All there is to do now is turn the wonderful roasted ingredients into a salsa. If using a blender, simply pulse until you reach desired consistency.

If you're processing by hand, a large pestle and mortar works great.

This salsa will keep in the fridge for up to one week. Store the salsa in an airtight container for maximum freshness.

Watermelon and Feta Salad with Glazed Walnuts

Prep time: 5 mins   **Cooking time: 5 mins**   **Serves: 4**

I can think of few salads as more-ish as this one. It's a complete celebration of different textures and flavours, combined into one giant party in your mouth. This is a fantastic, refreshing side to barbecued meats, or a wonderful light lunch on its own.

Equipment

- frying pan
- knife
- chopping board

Ingredients

- handful of walnuts
- 1 tbsp butter
- 2 tbsp honey
- half a bag of mixed salad leaves
- third of a cucumber, de-seeded, and cut into quarter chunks
- 300g watermelon, cut into inch chunks
- 50g feta
- half a lemon
- 1 tsp wholegrain mustard
- 3 tbsp olive oil

Method

The main work here is creating those glorious glazed walnuts, which will be little nuggets of absolute joy in your salad, I promise. Add walnuts to a dry pan, on medium heat, and let them toast a little. Keep stirring to prevent burning, with the high fat content they can catch quickly.

Once they start smelling nice and nutty, add butter to coat the walnuts. Next, add 1 tbsp honey and toss for 2 minutes. They'll look rich, shiny, and delicious! Leave the walnuts to cool.

Next, assemble the salad leaves, cucumber, and watermelon in a large dish. Crumble the feta over it with your hands. Then sprinkle over the warm, glazed walnuts.

Finally, you need to create the dressing. In a jug or bowl, add the juice of half a lemon, wholegrain mustard, 1 tbsp honey, olive oil, and lots of black pepper. Stir it up, drizzle all over the salad, and serve.

Apple and Ginger Summer Slaw

Prep time: 5 mins   **Serves: 4-6**

The volume of food that can be created by grating never ceases to amaze me! Coleslaw is one of my favourite ways to enjoy raw veggies, and this recipe lends itself perfectly to fresh summer dishes. Top your burgers with it and enjoy with barbeque meat… enjoy it with anything!

Equipment

- grater (mandoline, food processor, or box grater)
- garlic press
- large bowl
- wooden spoon

Ingredients

- 2 large carrots
- half a red cabbage
- 2 apples
- 1 red onion
- 2 garlic cloves, minced
- 1 inch fresh ginger, finely grated
- small handful fresh thyme, finely chopped
- 2 heaped tablespoons natural yoghurt
- 1 heaped tablespoon mayonnaise

Method

Grate carrots, cabbage, apple, and onion. Try to grate the carrots at 45 degree angles, to get strands that are neither too long nor too short. Add these to a large bowl, along with the minced garlic cloves, grated ginger, and thyme.

The next step is to spoon in the natural yoghurt and the mayonnaise. Enjoy the satisfying process of mixing it all together. Best served chilled.

Tip

Apples can hold a lot of moisture, depending on the variety. If your apples do this, squeeze the moisture from the grated pieces (using clean hands), before adding it to the mix, to prevent the slaw from becoming watery.

Perfect Spiced Potato Wedges

Prep time: 5 mins   **Cooking time: 36 mins**   **Serves: 2**

I don't care how far you've made it in life - every household needs a school dinner. Nostalgia is delicious! Sausages, beans, and these potato wedges are a popular treat in our home, more often than not, cooked with love by my husband. He is a particular enthusiast of the humble school dinner and wedges alike.

This is a versatile and tasty way to spice up potatoes. Method is everything for the perfect wedge!

Equipment

- chopping board
- knife
- pot
- colander
- baking tray

Ingredients

- 2-4 Maris Piper potatoes (depending on size), cut into wedges lengthways, with skins on.
- 3 tbsp olive oil
- 2 tsp mixed herbs
- 2 tsp smoked paprika
- 2 tsp garlic powder
- 2 tsp onion powder

Method

Preheat your oven to 180c. To make wedges, cut your potatoes in half, lengthways. Make diagonal slices with each half, to create wedges. You should get 3-4 wedges out of each potato half, depending on its size.

Add the wedges to salted, boiling water, and boil for 11 minutes until cooked through but not reduced to mush (there's an art to this, 11 minutes seems to be the perfect time!) Drain the wedges in a colander, and allow it to rest for 5 minutes to get rid of the steam.

Return to the (empty) pot and toss carefully with oil, mixed herbs, smoked paprika, garlic powder, and onion powder.

Line up the wedges on the baking tray, keeping it very evenly spaced. It is important that the tray is not crowded, as space is what is going to give you lovely crisp wedges.

Bake for 25 minutes until the wedges are golden and gloriously crispy.

When cooking roast potatoes it's important to measure out the correct amount in relation to how many people are eating...

...and then add a good few more. Because that's how many you'll really need.

Halloumi Fries

Prep time: 5 mins   **Cooking time: 10 mins**   **Serves: 4**

These are light and crisp on the outside, and soft and squeaky on the inside. They are smothered in cool, fruity flavours. This is the perfect vibrant side! I just love these doused in plenty of lime juice. They also make a fantastic group snack, especially washed down with a beer or two.

Equipment

- chopping board
- knife
- bowl
- frying pan
- wire rack

Ingredients

- 240g halloumi
- 80g plain flour
- 1 tsp smoked paprika
- 1 tsp garlic powder
- 1 tsp mixed herbs
- 200ml rapeseed oil
- 200ml natural yoghurt
- zest and juice of 1 lime
- half pomegranate
- half bunch coriander

Method

Cut halloumi into uniform sticks, about 1.5 cm thick. In a bowl, stir together flour, smoked paprika, garlic powder, and mixed herbs. Toss the halloumi sticks into the flour mix, until evenly coated on all sides.

In a frying pan, heat up the rapeseed oil on medium high heat, until it is 175c. This should take a few minutes. Add 4 halloumi sticks at a time to keep the temperature of the oil high (cool oil means soggy fries!) Shallow fry for 1-1.5 minutes on each side, until golden brown.

Remove the cooked fries and place on a wire rack. You may want to keep these warm in the oven at 70c while the rest of the batch cooks.

Add natural yoghurt to a serving bowl, and grate in the zest of lime. Stir, and top with a sprinkling of smoked paprika and cracked black pepper.

Serve halloumi fries drizzled in some of the natural yoghurt dressing, with wedges of lime, and a smattering of pomegranate seeds and chopped coriander.

Tip

Halloumi is a very salty cheese, so beware of adding additional salt, as you usually might add, or you'll throw the flavours off balance.

Charred Pineapple Salsa

Prep time: 5 mins   **Cooking time: 7 mins**   **Serves: 2**

I don't know who first discovered that flavour skyrockets when you cook a fruit or vegetable until the outside turns black, but I would like to shake their hand. This salsa is full of fresh, happy flavours, with a punchy infusion of smoky, blackened pineapple. It's especially delicious with white fish or chicken.

Equipment

- chopping board
- knife
- griddle pan or frying pan
- bowl

Ingredients

- 1 red onion, finely diced
- juice of half a lime
- 1 tin pineapple, cut into 1cm size pieces
- 1 pack vine ripened tomatoes, chopped
- coriander, roughly chopped
- finely chopped red chilli, to taste

Method

Begin by adding onion to a bowl with lime juice and give it a stir so it's evenly coated. The lime juice is going to sweeten the onion, so leave that to sit while you get working on the pineapple.

In a hot griddle pan or frying pan, add the pineapple with a dash of rapeseed oil - just enough to lightly coat the pieces. Toss the pineapple regularly until the outside begins to char, and don't be shy, let it get nice and caramelised. Once nicely charred, add to the bowl with the onion, and add the tomatoes. Stir in the coriander and chilli. Finish with a little olive oil to bring the ingredients together and make them shine.

Balsamic and Lemon Potato Salad

Prep time: 5 mins   **Cooking time: 25 mins**   **Serves: 2**

I love the unapologetic punch that this delivers to the taste buds. This potato salad doesn't follow the rules of creamy and mellow. This one is bold and full of texture. I promise you, it is absolutely more-ish and works year round!

Equipment

- knife
- chopping board
- large pot
- colander
- baking tray
- large bowl
- wooden spoon
- zester

Ingredients

- 200g new potatoes, halved
- 3 tbsp balsamic vinegar
- 2 tbsp rapeseed oil
- 1 tbsp mayonnaise
- 2 large shallots, finely diced
- zest of 1 lemon
- 30g grated parmesan

Method

Preheat your oven to 190c. In a pot of salted, boiling water, parboil potatoes until nice and tender when pricked with a knife. Drain, and add to a tray with the balsamic vinegar and rapeseed oil. Coat the potatoes evenly and season generously.

Roast in the oven for 20 minutes. The potatoes will turn a glorious, rich, golden brown with lovely dark bits from the balsamic.

Add the hot potatoes to a bowl and stir in the mayonnaise, shallots, lemon zest, and grated parmesan. Serve warm.

Ultimate Roast Potatoes

Prep time: 5 mins   **Cooking time: 50 mins**   **Serves: 4**

This is the crowning glory of any roast, the nostalgic staple - the old faithful. Once you nail the roast potato, your meals are forever elevated. My tried and tested method produces perfect roast potatoes that are soft and creamy inside, with a sweet and salty crunchy coating. Reserve these for when you want to show off!

Equipment

- peeler
- knife
- chopping board
- large pot
- colander
- baking tray
- zester
- tongs

Ingredients

- 500g Maris Piper potatoes, peeled and halved, or quartered (to get even sizes)
- 450ml chicken stock
- 2 tbsp lard, cut into 1 inch cubes
- 1 tbsp rapeseed oil
- 2 tbsp balsamic vinegar
- 2 tbsp fresh rosemary, finely chopped
- zest of 1 orange.

Method

Pre-heat your oven to 220c. Add potatoes to a pot filled with chicken stock (already brought up to temperature), and if needed, top with a little water to fully cover the potatoes. Boil for 7-10 minutes until they are 90% cooked (a knife should easily cut through the potato, with just a little resistance). Drain into a colander and toss until the outside looks agitated and fluffy; this is how you get crispy bits! Set aside while you prepare the fat and flavour.

To a baking tray, add lard, rapeseed oil, balsamic vinegar and rosemary. Place in the oven for 5 minutes, until the oil is very hot. Carefully remove the tray and add the potatoes. Turn them in the oil, coating them, and season very generously with salt and pepper. Ensure the potatoes are evenly spaced in the tray; no potatoes should be touching. Return to the oven and roast for 40 minutes, until they are a rich golden brown and look beautifully crisp. Be sure to take them out halfway, to turn.

Finish with a zesting of orange.

Tip

Tongs work better than a spoon for turning each potato, to ensure they are evenly coated in fat and seasoning.

Tenderstem Broccoli and Butterbean Salad

Prep time: 5 mins   **Cooking time: 3 mins**   **Serves: 2-4**

Either as a side dish or a light bite, this one is clean, cool, and colourful. This is a handy dish for barbeques or a meal with plenty of sides. I love beans, and my favourite of them all is the butterbean. I think there's something extremely satisfying about the way a fork plunges into them.

Equipment

- chopping board
- knife
- saucepan
- bowl
- wooden Spoon
- colander

Ingredients

- 1 bunch of tenderstem broccoli
- half red onion, finely diced
- 2 tbsp olive oil
- juice and zest of half lemon
- ½ tsp oregano
- 1 tin of butterbeans
- parmesan for shaving

Method

Cut broccoli into 1 inch pieces (cut at an angle to make it pretty). Add to a saucepan with salted, boiling water, for 3 minutes, until tender enough for a fork to prick them. The aim here is green veggies with plenty of bite; no soggy broccoli in your salad!

Add finely diced onion to a bowl with olive oil, lemon juice and zest, oregano, and butterbeans. Give them a good stir. Once the broccoli is cooked, drain, and add to the bowl.

Use a grater or peeler to shave slices of parmesan into the bowl. I haven't given a measurement for the cheese –measure with your heart! The parmesan will add plenty of salty flavour, add to taste, and stir in gently. Serve and enjoy.

"Wow! I've never known a girl who likes her food as much as you do!"

Oh yeah. I've heard that one a lot throughout my adult life. An unapologetic love of food always seems to strike a unique chord, particularly with men. I haven't found the tone to be disapproving, but rather one of fascination, perhaps because it's perceived to be uncommon.

And that's the thing, isn't it? We're not supposed to admit it. We're meant to pretend that we aren't too fussed; that we always want the salad and never the fries. And if we do indulge, we better make a big song and dance about how guilty we feel about it (don't get me started on that pig emoji).

Yawn. No thank you. If someone points out how much I'm enjoying my food I don't feel ashamed, I grin and take another bite. You better believe I'm enjoying it!

I know exactly what I want in every other aspect of my life and I'm not afraid to go for it. Why shouldn't it be the same with food? Don't spend your whole life ordering the salad and waiting to be offered the fries.

FOOD DIARIES: St Lucia

Alex and I are incredibly lucky (friends would prefer to call us jammy) that Alex's parents live in St Lucia, and so for the last fourteen years we've taken regular trips over to visit the beautiful island.

Every time I visit St Lucia I start the holiday the same way: a little pissed off (bear with me).

It's an odd one. It's as if you bring this little cloud along with you, a cloud that you perhaps didn't even know was there, until you air it out in the sunlight. It's an amalgamation of alarms and deadlines; of career analysis and five year plans. It is years and years of saving for the next big milestone. It's worrying that you aren't achieving those milestones fast enough. It's the everyday responsibilities and impatient aspirations that secretly stress you out, without you realising it... until you take some time to step back.

We all know it. Honestly, there's no place I've experienced on the planet yet, that's a better location to unwind than St Lucia. The problem is, I arrive in fast-paced, UK mode. The first few days I'm an uptight little English ball, getting annoyed at the traffic that's slowing me down, or wondering what I've forgotten to do as I lie on the beach, or thinking that I must get out of bed because... because I need to... I've got to do... nothing. I have got to do nothing.

It takes a while for my brain to adjust. Later, it hits me like one of those big waves in the Atlantic. I can physically feel myself melt into relaxation mode. This happens during every visit. On my last trip, it happened while I sat on a little rockery with a glass of rum in my hand. I had slipped away from the group at the beach barbeque, and found myself a little spot looking out onto the ocean. After zoning out for some time, I turned around to find a local man sat nearby doing the same thing.

"How are you enjoying the island?" he asked me with this slow, knowing smile, like he'd seen people having 'the moment' many times before.

Once you've entered the St Lucian holiday mode, responsibilities of home suddenly feel very far away. Life resets to what life should be about in the first place. Priorities become good conversation around the barbeque, resting to the sound of the waves in bed (oh, hearing the ocean in bed is so enjoyable), finding the sweetest coconuts from roadside vendors, and searching for fresh mangoes that freely scatter the island. What a wonderful place to remind yourself about the most important things in life: good food and good people.

FOOD DIARIES: *St Lucia*

FOOD DIARIES: *St Lucia*

MEAT

Orange and Garlic Chicken Legs

Prep time: 5 mins + 4 hours marinating   **Cooking time: 35 mins**   **Serves: 4**

This recipe is not only big on flavour, it'll fill your kitchen with the spectacular smell of caramelised orange. It's heavenly! This chicken recipe is hugely versatile and pairs wonderfully with salads for a light and fragrant meal. The prep work just takes a couple of minutes. It could not be easier, but for best results and maximum flavour, prep a few hours ahead of cooking time.

Equipment

- large bowl
- knife
- chopping board
- zester
- garlic press
- roasting tray

Ingredients

- 4 chicken legs with skin on
- 2 tbsp rapeseed oil
- 1 orange, juiced and zested
- 3 garlic cloves, minced
- 2 tbsp balsamic vinegar

Method

In a bowl, add the chicken, rapeseed oil, orange juice and zest, garlic, and balsamic vinegar. Mix well to coat the chicken and leave to marinate for 4 hours.

When ready to cook, place the chicken legs on a tray and roast in the oven for 35 minutes at 180c.

Once cooked, serve with a little more freshly grated orange zest over the chicken.

Tip

Place the fattest part of the chicken leg facing into the oven. This will help with even cooking and prevent dryness on the thinner parts.

Low and Slow Lamb Shoulder with Orzo

Prep time: 15 mins   **Cooking time: 4 hours**   **Serves: 6**

A rich and tender one pot wonder. This lamb melts off the bone after cooking for hours in a rich medley of vegetables and herbs. It's served with comforting orzo that has soaked up all the delicious lamb flavour. Total indulgence - I bet you've earned it!

Equipment

- knife
- chopping board
- garlic press
- wooden spoon
- large Dutch oven pot

Ingredients

- 2kg lamb shoulder
- 1 tbsp oregano
- 1 large white onion, diced
- 6 garlic cloves, minced
- 1 tbsp balsamic vinegar
- 2 red peppers, diced
- 200g plum tomatoes, halved
- handful fresh rosemary, finely chopped
- 1 tbsp cumin seed
- 2 bay leaves
- 500ml chicken stock
- 500g orzo

Method

Preheat your oven to 150c. Remove lamb from the fridge 30 minutes before cooking to bring it to room temperature. Season the lamb generously with salt & pepper.

On medium heat melt some olive oil in a Dutch oven, and add oregano. Place the lamb shoulder into the pot and fry for a few minutes each side, until the outside of the meat has browned. Remove the lamb from the pot and set aside for now.

Add onions and garlic to the pot. The cooked oregano and lamb juices that were released in browning the meat will smell incredible! Once the onions soften, add the balsamic to deglaze the pot, then add the red peppers and plum tomatoes, and stir well.

When the tomatoes soften, add the rosemary, cumin seeds, bay leaves, and the chicken stock. Stir well, and place the lamb on top. Spoon some of the juices over the lamb, then place the lid on and pop into the oven for 3 hours and 30 minutes.

When that time is up, remove the pot from the oven and temporarily remove the lamb - be careful as it may be starting to fall apart at this stage!

Pour your orzo into the pot and stir it into the delicious vegetable and stock mix. By now, it will have broken down into a beautiful rich sauce infused with the lamb juices. Return the lamb shoulder to the pot, place the lid back on and cook for a further 30 minutes.

Low and Slow Lamb Shoulder with Orzo

Tip

This dish really lends itself to family style dining –which is my favourite way to serve and eat food. Once cooked, remove the lamb from the pot and serve it on a platter. It's perfect as the centerpiece for your table. Watch the smiles light up on the faces of your diners! You can plate the orzo straight from the Dutch oven into dishes, and top with that meltingly tender lamb. I love the theatre of carving or pulling apart meat at the table!

This dish looks absolutely beautiful finished with a drizzle of natural yoghurt and a sprinkling of fresh parsley.

A Few of my Favourite Things

The soft crunch of a knife, chopping through chocolate.

Poking the top of an ultra soft brioche burger bun.

When the centre pith of a clementine comes out whole.

The rustle in the pan from a perfectly crisp roast potato.

The first spoonful, from a pot of extra thick cream.

The rasp of a spoon against an avocado skin.

The centre bite of a well-filled sandwich.

Spreading custard over a freshly set trifle.

The slow, methodical movement of a knife through a wedge of cheese.

Vibrating vision from really excellent crackling.

Watching butter melt into the holes of a crumpet.

The first dunk of crusty bread into baked camembert.

The sizzle of balsamic vinegar as it hits a hot pan.

The lingering smell of fresh thyme on your hands after cutting it.

Pricking an egg yolk.

Watching ice cream melt over the sides of a hot brownie.

Pan Fried Duck with Blackberry Sauce

Prep time: 5 mins   **Cooking time: 20 mins**   **Serves: 2**

Imagine soft and juicy meat, sweet and crispy fat, and a rich fruity sauce. This is such a treat and one of my favourite things to cook for myself on a weekend evening.

Equipment

- chopping board
- kitchen towel
- very sharp knife
- pan
- spoon
- heat proof bowl
- tongs
- baking tray
- wire rack
- wooden spoon
- grater

Ingredients

- 2 duck breasts
- 2 tbsp butter
- 2 shallots, finely grated
- 250ml chicken stock
- 2 glasses red wine
- 2 tbsp blackberry jam
- 2 sprigs fresh rosemary
- 150g fresh blackberries

Method

Preheat your oven to 170c. Start by prepping your duck breasts. Pat the skin with kitchen towel until dry. Take a very sharp knife, and score diagonal lines into the skin, about 5mm apart, then season very generously.

Heat a pan on medium heat. Once up to temperature, add the duck breasts skin side down. Allow them to cook for 5 minutes and do not move them around. No oil is needed as the skin is very fatty. To ensure a crispy skin you will need to tilt the pan and spoon off any excess fat. Do this repeatedly as the skin cooks.

After 5 minutes, when the skin is golden brown, flip the duck breasts and cook for 1 minute to seal the meat.

Remove from the pan and place onto a wire rack, skin side up, on a baking tray. Cook for 10 minutes. This will give you pink duck meat. Once cooked, allow to rest for 5 minutes.

While the duck is cooking, it's time to prepare the delicious sauce to accompany it. Return the pan to medium heat, add butter, and shallots. Stir regularly, until the shallots soften and are almost melted away.

Now add the chicken stock, red wine, and jam. Once the jam has melted, add the rosemary sprigs. Allow to reduce a little then add blackberries. Stir gently to keep the blackberries intact and continue to reduce until a rich sauce forms.

Duck looks wonderful served in slices when you can see the lovely blushing meat. Use a sharp knife to cut along the width and at an angle. Add to your plate and spoon over the glorious blackberry sauce.

Tip

I love to serve duck with really garlicky potatoes. In particular an extra buttery, garlic mash.

Spatchcock Chicken with Spring Onions and Clementines

Prep time: 5 mins   **Cooking time: 40 mins**   **Serves: 4-6**

Spatchcocking chicken can halve the cooking time of a regular roast chicken. It also makes it easy to carve up portions, plus I think it has a little more theatre to it. This recipe celebrates beautifully cooked, juicy chicken, infused with fragrant flavours. The perfect spring chicken dinner!

Equipment

- kitchen scissor
- roasting tray
- cooking brush
- zester
- knife
- chopping board

Ingredients

- 1 free range whole chicken
- 3 tbsp rapeseed oil
- 1.5 tsp garlic powder
- 4 clementines
- 1 red onion
- 4 spring onions

Method

Preheat your oven to 180c. Start by spatchcocking your chicken. Turn it over so that the underside faces you. Use kitchen scissors to cut along either side of the spine, to remove it.

Turn the chicken to face upwards again, and spread the carcass flat in a large roasting tray. Press down on the breast bone to flatten the meat. This is a surprisingly satisfying job.

Brush your chicken with rapeseed oil making sure that every part of the chicken is coated. The next step is to season generously with salt and pepper, and garlic powder.

Use a zester to grate the zest of the clementines over the chicken. Then quarter each clementine and place it underneath and around the chicken in the tray. Quarter the red onion and spring onion and place these around the bird evenly.

Roast for 40 minutes, with the largest part of the chicken breast facing into the oven. Remove when the juices run clear, and the chicken skin is a wonderful golden brown.

Serve with one final squeeze of the clementine segments over the chicken and enjoy!

Tip

Don't throw away the spine. It can be used to make a delicious homemade chicken stock, check out page 115.

Sticky Chinese Style Pork Belly

Prep time: 5 mins   **Cooking time: 65 mins**   **Serves: 4**

Give me this pork dish, basmati rice and pak choi, and I could happily eat it every day for the rest of my life. It's absolute heaven! A real crowd pleaser too. Watch eyes light up as this is served at your table!

Equipment

- chopping board
- knife
- garlic press
- pot
- Dutch oven pot
- colander
- wooden spoon

Ingredients

- 500g pork belly, sliced into 1cm chunks
- 1 tbsp sesame oil
- 2 tbsp demerara sugar
- 1 tbsp dark soy sauce
- 1 tbsp light soy sauce
- 1 tbsp mirin rice wine
- 1/2 tbsp rice vinegar
- 2 cloves garlic, minced
- 1 inch fresh ginger, minced
- 1 cup chicken stock

Method

Boil the sliced pork belly in a pot for 3 minutes then remove from heat and drain. Set aside.

In the empty pot, add the sesame oil on medium heat. Once up to temperature, add sugar and caramelise with the oil.

Once melted, add pork and stir for 2 mins until a little browned. Add the soy sauces, mirin, rice vinegar, garlic, and ginger, stirring well to combine. Add the chicken stock and simmer on very low heat with the lid on, for 1 hour.

Stir every 10-15 minutes. The liquid will reduce into a lovely, sticky sauce. You can add a little water if it gets too thick.

Serve on top of sticky basmati rice with pak choi. Be sure to spoon over lots of that lovely sauce as well!

Quick and Easy Chicken Nuggets

Prep time: 5 mins   **Cooking time: 15 mins**   **Serves: 2**

Who said chicken nuggets had to be junk food? This version is breaded, not battered, and baked, not fried. They're super speedy and make a tasty midweek protein or snack. Why not enjoy with potato wedges (page 79) and a fresh summer slaw (page 76).

Equipment

- knife
- chopping board
- bowl
- garlic press
- wooden spoon
- baking tray

Ingredients

- 2 chicken breasts, cut into large, chicken nugget size pieces
- 1.5 tbsp rapeseed oil
- 2 garlic cloves, minced
- 1 tbsp mixed herbs
- 1.5 tsp smoked paprika
- 60g panko bread crumbs

Method

Preheat your oven to 170c. In a bowl add chicken pieces. Now coat them evenly with rapeseed oil, garlic, mixed herbs, smoked paprika, and breadcrumbs.

Add to a baking tray with even gaps between the pieces.

Bake for 15 minutes.

Tip

Panko is a lovely, light, and crispy breadcrumb, but you can use any you like. If you have some stale bread to use up don't throw it out. Instead, cut the crusts off and blitz the stale bread in a processor. You can lightly toast the pieces in a pan with a little oil to add more colour and flavour. Store it in an airtight container with a little rice at the bottom, to keep the breadcrumbs dry and crisp.

Sweet and Herby Roast Leg of Lamb with Hasselback Potatoes

Prep time: 10 mins + 6 hours marinating　　**Cooking time: 1 hour 10 mins**　　　**Serves: 6**

This is a fantastic one-tray dinner. It has all the heartiness of a roast, but with a sweet infusion. It's a lovely, lighter roast dinner that I think is ideal for the warmer months of the year.

Equipment

- roasting tray
- knife
- chopping board
- garlic press
- large spoon
- pot
- colander
- foil

Ingredients

- 1.5kg half leg of lamb, bone on
- 2 tbsp olive oil
- 2 tbsp honey
- 2 tbsp balsamic vinegar
- juice of half lemon
- 3 garlic cloves, minced
- 3 sprigs fresh rosemary, finely chopped
- 3 sprigs fresh thyme, finely chopped
- 800g baby potatoes
- 3 sprigs mint

Method

Start by marinating the lamb. Prepare 6 hours before cooking to allow the flavours to infuse for best results.

Add lamb to a large tray and coat well in olive oil, honey, balsamic vinegar, and lemon. Once well coated, place it top side up, and rub the minced garlic, chopped rosemary, and thyme over the top of the lamb. Coat evenly.

Cover lamb and leave to marinate. When ready to roast, preheat your oven to 180c.

Now prepare your hasselback potatoes. To do this, place a potato onto a large spoon, and with a sharp knife cut along the width of the potato until you reach the spoon. Repeat until you have thin slices running along the back of the potato.

Once the potatoes are sliced, add them to a pot of boiling water for 7 minutes to take the edge off their rawness. They should feel tender when pricked with a knife. Carefully drain and allow them to dry off for a few minutes.

Place the hasselback potatoes around the leg of lamb, being sure to evenly coat them all in the marinade, which will collect in the bottom of the tray. Season well and place the mint leaves on top of the potatoes. This will add a light infusion when cooking.

Cook the lamb and potatoes for 50 minutes covered with foil, then 20 minutes uncovered.

I like to enjoy this lighter, sweeter version of a lamb roast, with oven roasted tomatoes left on the vine. Their natural sweetness works perfectly with this dish. Of course, gravy will never go amiss! Try adding some mint and a spoonful of jam to your gravy to further compliment the flavours of the dish.

Sweet and Herby Roast Leg of Lamb with Hasselback Potatoes

Tip

That half lemon that you squeezed over the lamb; don't throw it away! Add it to the tray while you roast. It'll steam and add more flavour to your meal, plus your kitchen will smell amazing!

HOW TO MAKE CHICKEN STOCK

The best thing about homemade stock is that it can be made of stuff that was heading for the bin. Leftovers and boiling water, plus a little extra flavour is all you need. It doesn't get easier or more cost effective than that.

I love to make chicken stock which has a subtle savoury flavour and lends itself perfectly to so many dishes. You need three key elements to make your stock:

Meat Base

Leftover chicken bones are the foundation of a good chicken stock. It can be the carcass of a roast chicken, the bones from barbecued legs, or the spine removed from a spatchcocked chicken. Whatever it is, don't throw it in the bin! Homemade stock is a wonderful way to reduce waste.

Vegetables

Vegetables add depth of flavour. Try to pick vegetables with some aroma. Onions and celery are particularly good for this purpose. Simply halve or quarter them for cooking.

Herbs and Fragrance

This is crucial for that extra infusion of flavour. Fresh bunches of thyme, rosemary, garlic, and cloves all make valuable contributions. Be sure to keep these ingredients whole, rather than chop them up. This makes for easy removal, once you're done cooking.

Cooking Your Stock

Simply place the ingredients into a pot and cover with boiling water. Simmer on the lowest heat for 1-2 hours until the water has reduced and turned a rich golden colour. Keep your stock in the fridge and use it within one week.

I do not believe that homemade stock should be an exact science - the beauty of a good stock is how versatile and care free it can be! Enjoy using the leftovers that you have at hand, and your intuition to experiment with different flavours and ratios.

Add stock to cooking potatoes, soups, stews, rice, and so much more. Where you might have used water - use stock and watch how your cooking intensifies!

There is magic in the mundane.

Big events, lifetime achievements, and dream purchases, are of course unforgettable, joyful episodes in our lives. The thing is, they don't happen often enough. Life is mostly composed of everyday occurrences, the seemingly forgettable moments that don't make their way into our core memories as specific happy events, but more as a general feeling.

Close your eyes and think of a decade that you adored. Perhaps it was the 80's or the 90's? Maybe there was that one amazing summer. There's a 'feeling' that comes with remembering that era, right? You can't pinpoint it to a specific event, instead it's just there – intangible, and built up of innumerable micro-moments of textures, sights, smells, and emotions.

Most of our time on this earth is made up of micro-moments, and most of them are unglamorous, consisting of maintenance, chores, work, and basic living. If we cannot find joy in the mundane - the filler between those explosive moments - then I think lasting happiness can be hard to find.

I believe that food can be that everyday magic. It is an opportunity every day to create a little slice of that 'feeling'.

A good meal will always bring joy.

BAKES AND DESSERTS

Chocolate Meringues with Raspberry Cream

Prep time: 15 mins   **Cooking time: 30 mins**   **Serves: 6**

This is a beautiful looking, light dessert. It combines deliciously sweet, fresh raspberry cream, with fresh berries, and is crowned with a show-stopping chocolate meringue.

Equipment

- 3x bowl
- electric whisk
- wooden spoon
- chopstick or skewer
- baking tray
- silicon mat or greaseproof paper
- piping bag

Ingredients

For the chocolate meringues:

- 3 egg whites
- 150g caster sugar
- 50g dark chocolate

For the raspberry cream:

- 300ml double cream
- 1 tsp vanilla extract
- 300g fresh raspberries

Method

Preheat your oven to 140c. In a bowl, whisk the egg whites until white and foamy. Next, whisk in the sugar little by little until stiff peaks form. You can rub some meringue in between your fingers to check if the sugar has dissolved. If it feels grainy, you must whisk some more. Once ready, set aside.

Melt chocolate either in a bowl over boiling water or in the microwave. This is the fun part! Use a spoon to drizzle melted chocolate into the meringue mixture. Then using a chopstick or skewer, swirl the chocolate around to create swirls of chocolate through the meringue.

Line a tray with a silicon mat or greaseproof paper and carefully heap a big tablespoon of the mixture onto the tray. Leave about two inches between each meringue.

Cook for 30 minutes and set aside to cool.

Now it's time to make the raspberry cream!

In one bowl, whisk double cream and vanilla together until soft peaks form. In another, mash most of the raspberries into a chunky coulis, setting aside about 80g for garnish. Add the mashed raspberries to the cream, and give the mixture one final whisk, until a stiff whipped cream forms.

Presentation time!

Add cream to a piping bag. In the centre of a dessert plate, pipe a generous mound of fresh raspberry cream. Line the outside of the cream with a circle of fresh raspberries. Finally, crown the raspberry cream with a show-stopping chocolate meringue.

Tip

When making the meringue mixture, take your time when adding the sugar. Dumping it in all at once knocks the air out of the mixture, which can create hollow meringues.

Spiced Apple Fritters with Cinnamon Glaze

Prep time: 10 mins   Cooking time: 15 mins   Serves: 4-6

These apple fritters are the doughnut's rustic, fruity cousin. Get ready for sweet chunks of spiced apple pieces enveloped in soft dough with a crispy shell, then dipped in a cinnamon glaze... a sweet tooth's paradise! They are absolutely more-ish and wonderful served hot with vanilla ice cream.

Equipment

- peeler
- chopping board
- knife
- frying pan
- wooden spoon
- large bowl
- whisk
- zester
- sieve
- large pot
- thermometer (optional)
- medium bowl
- kitchen towel
- wire rack

Ingredients

For the spiced apples:

- 1 tbsp butter
- 3 apples, peeled and diced into half-inch chunks
- 1 tsp cinnamon
- 1 tsp ground ginger
- 1 tsp ground nutmeg

For the batter:

- 1 egg
- 50g caster sugar
- 1.5 tsp baking powder
- zest and juice of 1 orange
- 100g plain flour
- 1 small jar coconut oil, for frying

For the cinnamon glaze:

- 3 heaped tablespoons icing sugar
- 1 tsp cinnamon

Method

Heat the butter in a pan on medium heat. Once melted, add the diced apples. Stir for a minute then add the cinnamon, ginger, and nutmeg. Continue to stir for 3-5 minutes until the apples soften. Your aim is to warm the apples and take the raw edge off them, but not to cook them into a soft mush. They must remain as apple pieces!

Once suitably soft, remove apples from heat. Set aside to cool a little while making the batter.

In a large bowl, whisk together the egg and sugar. Next, add the baking powder and orange zest and juice. Now, stir again. Pour in the apples and stir until they are coated in the wet mixture. Finally, sift in the flour and stir until you have a smooth, thick mixture.

Now it's time to fry the fritters. In a deep pot, add coconut oil and heat on medium. The temperature should reach 190c.If you have a thermometer, great stuff, but if you don't, it should reach this temperature in about 4-5 minutes, depending on your pot. Drop a little dough in to test: if it sizzles, the oil is ready.

Take heaped tablespoons of the mixture and carefully place it into the oil. Flatten out the top with the back of a spoon to create rough oval shapes. This mixture really expands, so only fry two at a time. The batter needs to reach a rich golden brown on each side, for that delicious crispiness. 1-1.5 minutes should do the trick. Remove them from the oil and set onto a kitchen towel to dry and cool.

Glaze time!

In a bowl, add icing sugar and cinnamon. Add teaspoons of cold water, 2 spoonfuls at a time, until you have a consistency that is quite runny. It should fall slowly but freely off a spoon. You want a glaze rather than a thick icing. Dip the fritters into the glaze and let dry on a wire rack. Finish with a generous dusting of icing sugar to make the fritters pretty (optional).

Mango and Lime Cream Pudding

Prep time: 5 mins   **Serves: 2**

This is a dessert for when you want dessert without the faff of making dessert. One to satisfy a sweet tooth, this little number is fresh and fruity with minimal ingredients. It'll give you something sweet in no time at all!

Equipment

- chopping board
- knife
- bowl
- whisk

Ingredients

- 1 mango, finely diced
- 200ml double cream
- 1 lime
- 4 ginger snap biscuits, smashed into large crumbs

Method

In a bowl, whisk cream until soft peaks form. Add the lime zest and squeeze half the juice in. Whisk a little more until suitably whipped.

To a small dessert dish or glass, add layers of diced mango and lime cream, scattering in ginger biscuit crumbs here and there, of course saving some for the top as well.

Grab a spoon and dive in.

Tip

Limes can be stingy with their juice. Persuade them by giving them a vigorous roll on your countertop before slicing and squeezing. Go wild: throw it against a wall for good measure! The activity will bring extra flavour to your food and be a stress release all in one go. Win, win!

Chilli Chocolate Mousse

Prep time: 10 mins + 6 hours chilling **Serves: 4**

Mousse is such a decadent tasting dish and yet it is surprisingly light, with only a few ingredients required. My chocolate mousse comes with a warming background hum of chilli. It's such a lovely sensation!

Equipment

- 2 large bowls
- electric whisk
- pot
- hand whisk
- wooden spoon

Ingredients

- 8 egg whites
- 40g brown sugar
- 170g dark chocolate
- ½ tsp cayenne chilli powder

Method

In one of the bowls, add the egg whites. Whisk with electric whisk until a white foam forms. Now slowly whisk in the brown sugar, and continue to whisk until stiff peaks form. Try the over-the-head test to know they're ready!

In another bowl, break up the chocolate. Place this over a pot of boiling water to melt. Once the chocolate is melted, stir in the chilli powder. Remove from heat and allow to sit for 1-2 minutes (chocolate mixed with egg whites when fresh off the hob, could scramble them!)

Get ready to work quickly here!

Technique is everything for a successful mousse. Take one quarter of the egg whites and add to the chocolate mix, hand whisking vigorously until the chocolate and egg whites are combined and resemble a thick chocolate sauce. Now take heaped dollops of the egg whites (one at a time), and gently fold into the chocolate using a wooden spoon, until the mousse is fully combined.

Place in your dessert dishes and chill in the fridge for at least 6 hours.

Tip

When melting chocolate, pick a pot that is quite a bit smaller than the bowl you are melting the chocolate in. If they are similar sizes it can risk steam creeping over the sides of the bowl and mixing with the chocolate, which will ruin the texture.

Fudgy Banana Brownies

Prep time: 10 mins   **Cooking time: 45 mins**   **Serves: 12**

This is hands down one of my most popular recipes, to date. If you adore brownies with incredible levels of goo, then this recipe is right up your street! Indulgent and rich with a banana infusion, these brownies celebrate natural sweetness and unapologetic fudgy texture.

Equipment

- large bowl
- wooden spoon
- small bowl
- fork
- wooden spoon
- sieve
- square 20cm baking tin
- greaseproof paper

Ingredients

- 140g butter, melted
- 80g cocoa powder
- 150g caster sugar
- pinch of salt
- 1 tsp vanilla extract
- 2 eggs
- 4 tbsp honey
- 3 very ripe bananas (2 mashed, one sliced for topping)
- 60g plain flour

Method

Preheat your oven to 180c. Line a square baking tin with greaseproof paper.

Add melted butter to a large bowl and sift in cocoa powder. Add sugar, salt, and vanilla. Stir well until fully combined. Next, add the eggs and stir thoroughly once more. Once fully combined add the honey... and stir some more.

Now it's time to mash your bananas!

Add two bananas to a small bowl and mash with a fork. Make sure not to mash them into a completely smooth paste. Some texture is good in this recipe and adds to the banana flavour. Add the mashed bananas to the batter and stir in. You will have a dark and very shiny batter.

Sift in plain flour, ensuring it is free of lumps, and carefully fold in. Pour the lovely batter into your baking tin and even out the top with the back of a spoon.

The final step is to garnish the banana brownie. Slice a third banana lengthways, and place on top of the batter (sliced side up, it looks prettier!) Be sure to push them in a little.

Bake for 45 minutes. Best enjoyed fresh from the oven.

Tip

Unlike cakes, when you test how baked a brownie is with a skewer, it should never come out clean. This means it is overdone! When testing, the skewer should be covered in a nice moist crumb.

Clean as you go...

I'd love to say I have a groundbreaking secret to stress free cooking, but the truth is my biggest tip for enjoying your time in the kitchen isn't very glamorous or exciting at all. It is simply this: clean up after yourself! I cannot stress the difference this makes to your cooking experience. It really will keep your time in the kitchen fun and relaxed, which is exactly what it should be!

I learnt this as a child when I attempted my very first cake.
Chaos ensued.
No surface was free of batter.
Cocoa powder went everywhere (everywhere)!
I cried.

Now I live and breathe this mantra. If like me, you have a small kitchen then it's even more important. Spend some time before you start to cook by clearing the dishwasher or sink. Arrange the equipment you need. Then, as you cook and complete tasks, remove scraps of food, wipe down surfaces, and put away used ingredients. It might feel tedious, but if you get into a groove of dancing around cleaning up after yourself, you'll be amazed how much faster and carefree your cooking becomes.

Classic Lemon Curd Cake

Prep time: 10 mins   **Cooking time: 30 mins**   **Serves: 12**

I just adore baking with lemons, and I love the colour even more. Any cake is good of course, but that lovely bright yellow just lifts my mood. It's perfect for a treat with loved ones! This cake with its moist, lemon zest sponge, rich lemon buttercream, and thick, tangy lemon curd, really celebrates that zingy flavour. It's an absolute joy on a cake stand!

Equipment

- 2x 20cm cake tins
- greaseproof paper
- 2 large bowls
- electric whisk
- sieve
- wooden spoon
- wire rack
- small bowl
- palette knife

Ingredients

For the sponge:

- 250g butter
- 250g caster sugar
- 4 eggs
- 2 tsp vanilla extract
- zest of 2 lemons
- 1 tsp baking powder
- 250g self raising flour

For the filling:

- 150g butter, softened
- 200g icing sugar
- juice of 1 lemon
- half a jar of lemon curd

Method

Preheat your oven to 180c and line the cake tins. In a large bowl, whisk together the butter and sugar until light and fluffy. Add eggs, vanilla, lemon zest, and baking powder. Mix in thoroughly. Sift in flour and fold in gently with a wooden spoon. Distribute the lemon cake batter evenly between the two tins and bake for 30 minutes, or until a cocktail stick poked into the cake comes out clean. Once baked, remove from the cake tins and leave to cool on a wire rack. Wait until they are completely cool before you begin assembling the cake, or decorating it.

In a clean bowl make the lemon buttercream filling. Whisk together the butter and icing sugar, ensuring the butter is at room temperature and very soft. It must blend into a smooth, light and fluffy buttercream. Squeeze in the juice of 1 lemon and mix well.

Add a thick layer of lemon curd to the bottom half of the cake before topping with the fluffy buttercream. When filling the cake, be sure to get right to the edges with the lemon curd and buttercream. Every bite of the cake should be full of delicious lemon flavour. Be sure to save enough buttercream to decorate the top of the cake too. A few large, heaped spoonfuls should do the trick!

Once a layer of lemon buttercream has been spread evenly on top of the cake, you can finish with some decoration. I love to use fresh lemon garnish as a true celebration of the flavour. Slice a lemon into very thin slices, you'll need 8 or 9 slices, and arrange them on top of your cake. You can use the leftover lemon that you zested. The slices are so thin that you won't notice the rind is missing a little yellow. No wastage!

Tip

Lemon curd can be ever so thick, so before spooning it onto the cake, add a teaspoon of water or two and stir it up until it has become a little more loose and easy to work with.

Bread Pudding

Prep time: 15 mins   **Cooking time: 1 hour**   **Serves: 12**

In my opinion bread pudding doesn't get the modern day credit it deserves. This traditional dessert creates a fruity, very moist tray bake and is a fantastic way to use up stale bread. Mine is also topped with a lovely crunchy crumble. You can enjoy it hot, or my personal favourite - cold from the fridge!

Equipment

- 20cm square tin
- greaseproof paper
- food processor
- 2x bowl
- wooden spoon
- small saucepan
- zester

Ingredients

For the bread pudding:

- 220g bread (no crusts)
- 350ml milk
- 100g butter, melted
- 80g demerara sugar
- 1 egg
- 100g sultanas
- 100g dried apricots, diced
- 50g dried cranberries, diced
- 2 tsp allspice
- zest of one orange

For the crumble:

- 25g cold butter, cubed
- 50g plain flour
- 25g demerara sugar

Method

Preheat oven to 170c. Line and grease a tin, and add bread to the food processor. Pulse until the bread turns into large breadcrumbs. Add the bread to a bowl, and pour the milk over it. Stir, and set aside to soak.

Melt the butter and pour over the bread crumbs. Next, add the sugar and stir. Add the egg, and stir thoroughly to combine and reduce lumps in the mixture. Next, add all of the fruit, allspice and zest. Stir once more. Once combined, pour into the tin and smooth out to create an even layer.

Now it's time to make the crumble topping!

In a clean bowl, rub together the cubed butter and flour until you have a light crumb, still with some larger chunks. Stir in the sugar. Sprinkle this over the bread pudding, pressing down into the mixture a little. Bake for 1 hour. Once cool, cut into squares.

Sticky Orange Loaf

Prep time: 10 mins   Cooking time: 40 mins   Serves: 8

This is sweet, sticky, and not too large. It's perfect for when you fancy cake, but don't have all hands on deck to tackle such a big one. Oranges always make the most incredible fragrance when they cook. The smell of this cake as it comes out of the oven is guaranteed to bring you a little joy! Not to mention how beautiful the deep golden colour is as well.

Equipment

- pound loaf pan
- greaseproof paper
- weighing scales
- large bowl
- whisk
- zester
- wooden spoon
- sieve
- small bowl
- pastry brush

Ingredients

- 150g softened butter
- 150 demerara sugar
- 3 eggs
- juice and zest of 1 large orange
- 2 tbsp sour cream
- 140g self raising flour
- ½ tsp baking powder
- 2 tbsp marmalade
- ½ tsp ground ginger

Method

Preheat oven to 180c. Grease the sides of a loaf pan and place some greaseproof paper along the base.

In a large bowl, whisk together the butter and sugar until a light and creamy texture forms. Now, whisk in the eggs. Add the zest and juice of the orange and the sour cream. Stir through until evenly combined. Sift in the flour and baking powder, using a wooden spoon to carefully stir it in. Spoon the mixture into the loaf pan and even out the top.

Bake for 40 minutes.

In a small bowl, mix the marmalade and ground ginger together. Mix it until the marmalade is broken down into a workable texture, to brush over the top of the cake.

Once baked, remove the cake from the oven and turn it out from the cake tin. While still hot, generously brush the top of the cake with the ginger marmalade glaze.

Tip

Whisking is fantastic for creaming together the wet ingredients, but switch to a wooden spoon once you begin to work in the flour. Overworking the cake batter will make the cake very dense.

Rum Raisin Fudge

Prep time: 15 mins + 6 hours marinating   **Cooking time: 30 mins**   **Serves: 18**

Fudge is the best. I love how creamy it is, and how many different flavours you can apply to it. It happily keeps for at least a week in an airtight container, so this is perfect to make in advance. It's great to have on hand when you fancy a treat with a cuppa. Fudge making is a workout, but worth it.

Equipment

- shallow dish
- deep pot
- wooden spoon
- culinary thermometer (optional)
- glass of ice cold water
- 20 x 20cm square tray

Ingredients

- 100g sultanas (I know, I'll explain)
- 150ml dark rum
- 110g unsalted butter
- 450g demerara sugar
- 130g whole milk
- 397ml (one can) condensed milk

Method

Right, I know I've called this rum and raisin because y'know, it's the classic, plus alliteration is sexy, but the thing is I just massively prefer sultanas. They're bigger and juicier. If you're a diehard raisin fan, then feel free to use them, but trust me with the sultana switch!

To make your rum soaked raisins (sultanas!) add them to a shallow dish and cover with the rum. Leave to soak for at least 6 hours. Overnight is preferable. Cover them with cling film and leave at room temperature to do their thing. The pool of rum will slowly disappear and your dried fruit will get plumper and plumper. Once they're done, you must try one - they're delicious!

When they're ready for the fudge making, drain off any small amounts of liquid that might not have soaked, and allow them to dry a little on the outside.

In your pot, add butter, sugar, milk, and condensed milk and heat on high. It will take a few minutes to melt down and come to a rolling boil. At this stage reduce the heat a tad. All you have to do now is stir continuously until the mixture reaches 115c. This will take 15-20 minutes… it's an arm work out!

Keep an eye on the mixture to make sure it doesn't burn or boil over. Continuous stirring will prevent both of these things. You can use the thermometer to see if the mixture is 115c, or take a teaspoon of the mixture and drop it into a glass of very cold water. If the mixture hardens into a fudge consistency, then it is ready.

When ready, remove the mixture from heat and begin to stir vigorously. After a few minutes, once the fudge has cooled a little, you can stir in the rum raisins. You need to stir for about 10 minutes, until the fudge cools and gets very thick. Plenty of stirring is super important for smooth fudge! Otherwise sugar crystals will form and your fudge will be gritty.

Rum Raisin Fudge

Once very thick and smooth looking, add to the tin and allow it to set. It should be ready to slice into bite size pieces in 20 minutes.

Tip

If your fudge is grainy, all is not lost. Simply break the fudge up into a pot, and boil down once more. Add a little splash of milk to help loosen it back up, and repeat the entire process. That stirring part is so important!

You were not put on this earth to feel guilty about satisfying a basic human need.

I believe that happiness is in living unapologetically. Living for you! We are all unique with different desires. Contrary to what society would have you believe, there is no one size fits all approach to life. So listen to your own mind regarding what you want, and for the love of God, no one else.

I think one of the biggest skills we can learn is to empower ourselves to be intuitive, and to go through life saying yes and no-thank-you with full conviction. Do you want dessert? Yes? Then do yourself a service and say it with confidence! No more asking around the table for what everyone else is doing.

And FYI, I'm definitely enjoying a dessert with you.

I really hope you enjoyed reading this book as much as I loved writing it. In purchasing this book, you have supported a dream, so thank you, from the bottom of my heart!

If you love your food and would like to keep up to date with new recipes, and what I very much hope will be future book releases, follow me on Instagram at @jogirleatsworld

You can also use my hashtag #cookiteatitliveit to share any recipes you try. I share all photos to my page!

Finally, you can also visit my blog at GirlEatsWorld.co.uk

GIRL EATS WORLD

by jo kenny

About the Author

Jo lives in Bedford with her husband Alex, baby son Callum and Kimchi the cat. Her website GirlEatsWorld.co.uk was founded in 2012. Starting out as a personal space to capture cooking and food experiences, it has evolved into a public hub for recipes, cooking guides and food inspiration. Jo is passionate about fresh ingredients eaten joyfully and intuitively.

To stay up to date with new recipes, content and upcoming book releases connect with Jo on social media:

@jogirleatsworld (Instagram / TikTok / Twitter / Facebook)

CPSIA information can be obtained
at www.ICGtesting.com
Printed in the USA
LVHW071907150322
713508LV00001B/1

* 9 7 8 0 6 2 0 9 5 5 2 7 0 *